Tributes
*&*Tirades

Taos Life and American Politics

I0098953

Tributes
&Tirades

Taos Life and American Politics

ROBERT J. SILVER

TRIBUTES AND TIRADES: TAOS LIFE AND AMERICAN POLITICS
Copyright © 2013 by Robert J. Silver
All rights reserved.

Printed in the United States of America.

No part of this book may be used or reproduced in any manner
whatsoever without written permission, except in the case of brief
quotations contained in critical articles or reviews. For more
information, contact Nighthawk Press at www.nighthawkpress.com.

ISBN: 978-0615807997
Library of Congress Control Number: 2013939513

Cover artwork: "Streaming," by Dianne Frost
"Send in the Clowns," by Stephen Sondheim, 1973

Cover and interior page design:
Lesley Cox, FEEL Design Associates, Taos, New Mexico
(www.feeldesignassociates.com)

Editing:
Bonnie Lee Black, Taos, New Mexico (www.bonnieleeblack.com)
Barbara L. Scott, Final Eyes, Taos, New Mexico (www.finaleyes.net)

Type is set in Stempel Schneidler.

NIGHTHAWK PRESS
TAOS, NEW MEXICO
www.nighthawkpress.com

For Ande, Madison, Emily, Zoë, and Beckett

Contents

American Politics

In Conclusion

Acknowledgments

First and foremost my gratitude goes to Dianne Frost. Not merely my wife and a talented visual artist, she has also been my informal in-house editor and truth-telling cheerleader/ critic. Dianne generously brings her complementary creativity to the written word in the cover art for *Tributes and Tirades.*

"Streaming," Dianne's original 20-inch by 30-inch acrylic on canvas and the cover image for *Tributes and Tirades* was stolen in a 2011 burglary of our home. Its digital retrieval offers a treasured evocative envelope for the writing that follows. The painting's reproduction also represents an effort to recapture, resurrect, reclaim, and restore this lost work. I am both honored and delighted with this pairing of our artistic efforts.

Then, there is the little jewel of an academic institution, the University of New Mexico at Taos, and its talented creative-writing faculty. Absent Steve Fox initiating my writing efforts, along with a series of Bonnie Lee Black's creative-nonfiction classes and writers' workshops, the current work could not exist.

Beyond being my teacher, my friend and an accomplished author, Black lent her editing expertise to this project. Her unflagging intellectual integrity could always be counted on. Indeed, clunkers that may remain in the following essays are most likely the result of my stubborn refusal to jettison those flawed "little darlings," words I had written and could not bear to part with, no matter how insistent my scrupulous editor may have been.

Barbara Scott's "final eyes" not only hunted down errant typographic and grammar crimes and misdemeanors, but also brought her keen intellect to bear, challenging the coherence of the final product's rhetoric.

Lesley Cox's design and Rebecca Lenzini's Nighthawk Press offered talented finishing expertise to the work.

The Taos News and its editor, Joan Livingston, were an accepting, responsive, and tolerant venue for initial publication of many of the pieces in this collection. Without this award-winning weekly's de facto collaboration, these essays would likely have remained unread except by a few close friends and family. Both *The Taos News* and her sister newspaper, *The Santa Fe New Mexican*, have my thanks for carrying the pieces that originally appeared in their Op-Ed pages. I also thank the literary journals *HOWL* and *Chokecherries* for publishing earlier versions of my writing.

I am grateful to my friends and acquaintances — those who have felt comforted and those who have felt afflicted by my recurrent written "rants." I am especially thankful for the generous spirits of those whose political opinions stand in stark contrast to my own. Their continued friendship is ongoing testimony to the proposition that our shared humanity unites us far more than our differing political views divide us. It is in this spirit of tacit agreement to agreeably disagree that the current collection is offered.

Finally, there is Taos itself. I shall be forever grateful to the rich, unique, creative milieu of people and place that is this town.

Prologue

Taos is unquestionably magical. Yet, in light of sometimes clownish elected officials, traffic-regulation indifference, ubiquitous unpaved roads, automobile yard art, stray dog packs, and unconventional business practices, life here is like a cross between a third-world banana republic and a Seinfeld episode. Nevertheless, Taos has been deeply and surprisingly transformative for many, including me.

For me that transformation began one radiant Sunday morning. Looking out toward Taos Mountain from a friend's living-room window, I felt something powerful shifting within me. Taos magic — our community's stunning mix of people and place, the heretofore unknown possibilities that are nurtured and evoked in the unsuspecting and perhaps even in the initially reluctant — began to work its will on me.

On that day in December 2009, a small group of friends had gathered for coffee and conversation in a Taos-area home. When our host read aloud from a piece in the *Christian Science Monitor,* a heated discussion ensued. The article seemed to suggest that President Obama was not accepted in some quarters as the legitimate president of the United States. The *Monitor* reported on so-called "prayers" being offered for our new president by some on the Christian right: prayers for our president's death.

Our small group of politically progressive friends were uniformly shocked, dismayed, and outraged by the dangerous hostility toward the president detailed in the news account. Could people of faith actually be praying for the death of an American president? Apparently they could, and indeed they were.

Over the ensuing days, I remained deeply troubled by the contents of this newspaper article. I churned in anguish at what I had heard over Sunday's coffee. I felt I could no longer remain silent, but how could I personally act in opposition to this unconscionable corruption of religious teaching? I could not stand passively by. But what could I, a single individual, do to oppose this outrage?

Somehow, my distress found its way to my computer keyboard. An essay, "For the Soul of a Nation," emerged. That piece soon appeared as a column in the Op-Ed pages of our local weekly, *The Taos News*. This became the first of dozens of subsequent essays published in that newspaper, along with a couple of Op-Ed columns in *The Santa Fe New Mexican*. The published pieces were a series of commentaries on national politics interspersed with episodic musings on life in our isolated mountain community.

Much to my surprise, I was off and running. Since then, I am continually prepared to "rant" in print about something or other. Indeed, my mostly unsolicited Op-Ed submissions tend to exceed the *Taos News*'s capacity to publish them. Their rule is 30 days between submissions. In the intervening time, I am invariably champing at the bit.

All of my pre-Taos writing had been the technical stuff of a 40-year career in clinical and forensic psychology: dry, precise, mind-numbing research reports; convention-dictated psychological evaluations; obsessively couched and qualified forensic opinions. It was the sort of writing that only a most determined reader would ever wish to penetrate.

Life history is always relevant, and mine was that of an acutely shy and uncommunicative child. I naturally sought refuge, comfort and safety in keeping my opinions to myself. This deeply ingrained inclination eventually became adaptive. It just happened to be an excellent fit for the opaque persona that is the norm in my clinical psychology profession. As a psychotherapist, one should generally not wear one's heart on one's sleeve, and I was already so inclined. The complementary combination of personal history and career-dictated reticence reinforced shunning mass-media expression of my private opinions — until Taos.

These essays are the result of writing that began on that day in 2009. It is an occasional but persistent series of "tirades" and "tributes," musings, reflections, reactions, and observations on subjects and events that have activated my often critical and sometimes laudatory voice.

As an acknowledged political junkie, my frequent subject has been national politics. However, I've also been moved to comment on the rich and complicated experience of Taos life and beyond. For better or worse, I seem to have adopted a personal mission to "comfort the afflicted, and to afflict the comfortable."

It has taken me a lifetime to publicly parade my often controversial opinions. A once shy, anxious child, I likely gain perverse pleasure in sticking my thumb in the eye of the comfortable, the secure and the powerful. It feels a bit like standing up to the neighborhood bully. My rants also connect me with still-silent kindred souls. Friends and acquaintances say that they know me more fully through my writing. Not surprisingly, I come to know myself better through my written words as well.

A saying among my psychotherapist colleagues is that in life there are no accidents. While this may not be literally true, it invites people to be curious regarding their unconscious contributions to their own misfortunes and predicaments. In effect, "We have met the enemy and he [or she] is us." In a similar vein, I ponder my own motivations for producing the essays that follow. I am certain that they, too, are no "accidents." As I write and reflect, perhaps my self-understanding will also deepen.

The "tributes" that follow were a special joy to express. They offer my deep gratitude for the unmerited gifts I have received, which I sometimes neglect to fully put into words. They convey my thanks to Taos's talented and stimulating people, and they record my reverence for the cherished gift of citizenship in a nation whose people are free to speak their minds.

Taos Life

Seeing the Light

The glittering glow of the late-afternoon sun invigorates me, warms my soul, and illuminates the return to our Taos home. I am again awestruck by this world apart from my Bronx beginning. Cresting the highway's horseshoe bend just south of town, the lit-up land shimmers and pulses before me. Its iridescent rays reach out, drawing me into intimate embrace, captivating my consciousness. It is like a longed-for lover drawing me to her treasured touch.

Words never do justice to the stunning spectacle. Borrowing from a famous Frank Zappa remark, writing about Taos's light is like "dancing about architecture." Words cannot adequately capture it. It must be lived.

Many have heard the fabled Taos transformational tale: A broken wagon wheel strands wandering early–20th century artists in an unfamiliar, enchanting land. The nomadic artists are stunned, enthralled, and "blinded" by this strange land's legendary light. They stay. Thus the Taos artist colony is born. Taos's art identity becomes more deeply ordained and solidified.

History does repeat itself. It's common to hear recent arrivals tell of being transfixed by the land's light, honeyed hues and purpled pastels. They speak of it in rapturous, reverent phrases.

Taos is much about art, and visual art is much about light. This land of legend beams varied forms of evocative and transformative light into the hearts and souls of its people. Its incubating, nurturing rays give birth to broad creativity, transforming both the willing and the wary. It may or may not be good news, but I'm a case in point.

Now semiretired and settled in Taos, I find myself enlarged and enlightened by my adopted land. I now seek a reading audience far beyond that of fellow professionals and academics. This energizing of a previously dormant interest was completely unexpected. Metaphorically, it's as if I've somehow "seen the light."

Writing on new subjects flows out of me now as if propelled by a previously unknown force. Taos has illuminated a part of me that I didn't know existed. It has tapped a parallel personal universe slumbering within.

Prior to my own "broken wagon wheel" move to Taos, my writing, as previously indicated, was tediously technical. As sleep-inducing and mind-numbing as it may have been, it was the type of writing required by the conventions of my clinical psychology profession.

Land, light, and legend notwithstanding, Taos has yet to cure me of a chronic affliction, a perverse penchant for prolix, pedantic, ponderous prose. Fortunately, Taos is also home to talented editors. They struggle valiantly to shine a curative light on my linguistic crimes and misdemeanors. Perhaps it's only one transformation per customer.

Nevertheless, hope lives. Taos works its will in strange, mysterious, and life-altering ways. Naïve nomads, beware!

Snatched from the Jaws of Death

"Snatched from the jaws of death…one more time" are the words that come to my mind after every Taos bike ride. Pedaling through town, I treat each automobile as a potential death threat. My friends think I'm crazy to bike in this town. They may be right.

I was somewhat bemused listening to cheerleaders for a recent "bike to work" day in Taos. They were extolling the joys and virtues of biking, apparently blithely unaware of the death-defying essence of this arguably innocuous form of recreation. These people may be traveling the roadways of a different world.

Though I ride vigilantly, the drivers with whom I "share" the road puzzle me. These motorized fellow travelers seem drawn to me like a magnet. I cannot imagine that they really intend to harm me. There must be some other explanation. So, as a matter of survival, I've tried to see our life-threatening encounters through their eyes, and I've come up with a few theories.

An earlier version of this essay appeared in the Op-Ed pages of *The Taos News* on June 10, 2010.

It's a case of mistaken identity. Though I am rather small in stature, I assume from their actions that these motorists have somehow mistaken me for an NFL defensive-end lookalike. They engage me as if I were possessed of such incredible physical prowess and indestructibility as to be a reasonable match for a several-thousand-pound automobile. Astride the saddle of my trusty bike, I must somehow loom large enough to delude motorists into thinking that I'm some indomitable hulk. If this keeps up, I may have to revise my self-image. Only then would this sort of man-versus-vehicle competition make sense.

It's my clothing. Women will probably sympathize with this theory. My garish biking outfit must be the problem. Could it be that my high-visibility yellow jersey is something like waving a red flag before an agitated bull? With a protective helmet added to my colorful outfit, I may be creating the aura of someone dressed for close military combat. Both combat troops and knights of yore would don helmets as they prepared to engage hostile forces. It must be that I am mistaken for a member of a bicycle-mounted alien assault brigade. Why else would motorists be trying to annihilate me? I always used to think that bike clothing looked pretty nerdy. Go figure.

It's the hand signals. Lacking electrical directional signals, bikers routinely employ hand signals unfamiliar to many motorists — especially the younger ones. In signaling a right turn, the convention is for the left arm to be extended forming a right angle at the elbow, with the forearm and hand held vertically. Prior to the advent of electrical directional signals, drivers routinely employed such hand signals. These signals may now be vestigial anachronisms.

In their apparent unfamiliarity with any kind of turn signal, hand or electrical, local drivers probably see my gesture as "flipping them off." Makes perfect sense. They get insulted. In response, they feel compelled to defend their sacred honors. Could they reasonably be expected to do less?

It seems that all these problems would be resolved if I could just make a few simple changes: obscure my unintentionally hulking and indestructible physical appearance, wear clothing that is less visible and self-protective, and refrain from signaling for turns. Motorists who are now trying to kill me might then be mollified. They would no longer feel terrified of the threat that I inadvertently represent. Their preemptive self-defense attacks would be unnecessary. There would be "[road] peace for our time."

Therefore, in consideration of the general welfare of the Taos community, I hereby pledge unconditional bicycle disarmament, offer repentance for my past menacing physical appearance, and promise that I will henceforth "give [highway] peace a chance." I surrender!

Then, just when I think I have things figured out, I unexpectedly encounter one of Taos's profoundly generous drivers, who is more protective of me than I am of myself. You know who you are. My family thanks you, my friends thank you, and I, to my dying day (no wisecrack intended), thank you.

Who Let the Dogs Out?

In the wee hours of the morning, one cannot help but see Taos in a different light. Although I have scrupulously adhered to my personal pledge of bicycle nonviolence, I am regularly confronted with yet another unanticipated biking threat. Who let the dogs out?

Consistent with a personal commitment to peaceful cycling, I have radically altered my seemingly provocative bicycle behavior. As a sign of my good faith and capitulation to the superior mechanized force of motor vehicles, I have generally withdrawn from traveling the streets of Taos during prime daylight hours. Instead, I've taken to riding before sunrise. If motorized minions and cyclists no longer share the same roadway, I figure there's less likelihood of dangerous encounters.

But despite my best pacifist efforts, I have come upon a new threat in the form of man's so-called "best friend," the four-legged masters of the darkened traffic-free streets. Dogs, I've discovered, rule the night.

As their human owners slumber through the early-morning hours, these furry charges may have misunderstood

An earlier version of this essay appeared in the Op-Ed pages of *The Taos News* on July 29, 2010.

the mission of our acequia majordomos, whom they obviously admire and seek to emulate. Though they are likely doing their best, these overeager creatures seem to have confused the flow of irrigation water with the flow of neighborhood bicycle traffic. Such nuances may easily elude them.

Yes, I know. I've heard it before: "Fido doesn't bite … won't hurt you … is just curious … ignore him." These are famous last words, indeed. Fido somehow inevitably develops a special taste for me!

Don't get me wrong. I like dogs. My wife and I happen to live with and love one, a cockapoo named Shadow, who's like a family member. The problem is that strange dogs apparently get to like me just a bit too much. If we were still living in Texas, I could more easily understand the whole thing. There, you see, by state statute the first bite is essentially free: no lasting harm, no foul.

I had always thought that New Mexico was a bit more relationship-conscious than Texas. Indeed, our welcoming local customs include a warm and enthusiastic *abrazo*. I have not known us to snarl at, charge, or bite one another on first contact. Perhaps I am not yet fully acculturated. I assumed that you really had to know someone quite well before you took familiar liberties and growled at or tasted the person.

As I become regularly acquainted with our neighborhood canine emissaries, it appears they are being just a little bit forward, a bit too familiar. Perhaps I'm old fashioned. Nevertheless, this close interaction with dogs I hardly know is going to take some getting used to.

I'm in something of a quandary. Surely my pained expression proves I don't bike merely for fun. Nor would I choose to do this for my health. However, my physician is a physically fit, six-foot-tall woman and a competitive martial-arts expert. I respectfully and affectionately refer to her (always behind her back) as the "exercise Nazi." She has decreed that increased aerobic exercise is a must in the treatment of my Parkinson's disease. Biking, she counsels, is a perfect solution to my aerobic deficit. She-who-must-be-obeyed is a neurologist and not an E.R. doctor.

I remain on the horns of a dilemma. I seem to have no good options. Do I continue to tempt these snarling dogs with my early-morning bicycling? Do I risk incurring the wrath of the exercise Nazi by giving up biking? The path forward is unclear. If it comes down to a choice, I wonder which would have the more damaging bite, the dogs or the doctor.

Strangers in a Strange Land

Life in Taos is anything but ordinary. For their own protection, visitors require some explanation of local customs in our little corner of the Land of Enchantment.

Despite Taos's well-known arts identity, tourists are probably surprised by the countless pop-art sculptures installed throughout town. These objects closely resemble traffic signs. They are large, red hexagonal pieces with white lettering and borders. All of them have identical big block letters: "S T O P."

A number of other public sculptures of the same genre are selectively installed in the most heavily traveled parts of town. These particular art objects contain lights — red, yellow, and green — sometimes mounted horizontally and sometimes vertically. Miraculously, they shine in the same fixed sequence at all hours of the day and night, 365 days of the year, in good weather and bad.

Newbies might mistakenly assume that these objects have something to do with our town's traffic control. Not so! They actually constitute the first wave of omnipresent pop art, installed as part of a long-rumored, all-encompassing program of art in Taos's public places.

An earlier version of this essay appeared in the Op-Ed pages of *The Taos News* on May 6, 2010.

You'll observe that most local drivers treat these devices as artsy curiosities, rather than as traffic-control authorities. The local custom is to respond to the signals emanating from these pieces of public art as if they were mere suggestions, rather than commands. We all know that only psychotics receive and obey commands from inanimate objects. On the other hand, maybe that's the problem with the drivers holding those little rectangular wireless electronic things up to their ears. They sure act as if they're hearing voices.

The same holds true for those other ubiquitous public sculptures: the white rectangles with the large embossed black numerals: 15, 20, 25, 30, 35. Pop art again. Outsiders presume that the numbers have something to do with speed limits, but we know better. They're mere suggestions. You know this is so from the fact that Taos drivers rarely match their speed to the numbers on the objects.

Then there are the drivers who come roaring up behind you and follow your car as closely as physically possible. Tailgating? Not so! In reality, these people are so powerfully overcome with curiosity that they are helpless to contain their compulsion to become acquainted with you. They intend no harm. Locally, we refer to them as "Roadrunners," after those congenitally curious but not terribly intelligent creatures, New Mexico's state bird.

Another quaint local custom involves the behavior of drivers on our most heavily trafficked thoroughfares. Tourists probably assume that a driver pulling out into moving traffic on a crowded roadway is required to yield to oncoming cars. Not so in Taos.

Anyone observing this local activity will note that our custom is the exact opposite. You may have to slam on your brakes or instantly swerve to avoid a collision. This is all part of our community-wide commitment to sharpening your reflexes. We assume you may have been drawn to Taos partly for its world-class skiing. It is our desire to make sure that you are in optimal condition to tackle the moguls on our expert slopes. Forcing you to instantly react to potential auto accidents is the best we can do to keep your skiing reflexes razor sharp. You've probably heard the old saying, "Whatever doesn't kill you will make you stronger." Amen.

Finally, there is a local custom that tourist-pedestrians and visiting bicyclists will especially need to understand. New Mexico traffic laws require that drivers defer to these non-motorized lower life forms. But in Taos, the local custom most assuredly is to not give these organisms an inch. If these pesky life forms are endangered or eliminated, so much the better. If we wipe them out, won't we have improved the gene pool?

So, dear tourists, and fellow travelers, I urge you to think of yourself as on safari. Taos can be a whole other universe.

The "Nazi" and Me

Enchanting though it may be, Taos does take some getting used to. So I probably shouldn't have been too surprised when I came up empty-handed on my very first trip to the local Department of Motor Vehicles.

I had come, as had legions of seekers before me, a prostrate supplicant in search of required replacements for my now suddenly contraband Texas plates. In my quest, I was at the mercy of the formidable forces of banal bureaucracy.

I had in my possession a reasonable and appropriate array of routinely required documents. I'd been through this before at other times and in other places: in Indiana, Kansas, Illinois, and Texas. How different could Taos be? Isn't it a part of the old U. S. of A.? Yes, I know, states have some pretty peculiar laws and regulations when it comes to alcohol and sex. But, this was just about license plates. There is not really much illicit pleasure to be found in screwing license plates onto a car bumper.

After a seemingly interminable wait, affording more than ample opportunity to observe the slow-motion conduct of the routine bits of business passing through the DMV office, it is my turn to approach a female official stationed behind the

An earlier version of this essay appeared in *HOWL: The Voice of UNM–Taos,* Fall 2010.

long office counter. I dutifully spread my sheaf of documents out before her. She studies my papers carefully…knowingly… critically.

This woman holds temporary power over me. Palpably unsympathetic, she seems determined to find some reason, any reason — no matter how arbitrary — to deny me my license plates. This is her fleeting moment of authority, and she's going to wield it without mercy.

I am incredulous. She's actually telling me that the morning trip has been for naught. Her Inspector Clouseau–like detective work has miraculously uncovered some totally trivial flaw in my paperwork. I've wasted all this time. She is not going to give me the goods. She is a dead ringer for the Seinfeld TV sitcom "Soup Nazi." The Taos equivalent of, "No license plates for you," reverberates through my consciousness.

I am still unclear regarding the depth of primitive ire that this futile waste of time evoked in me. That understanding may be for another day. Perhaps, I was just having a bad day.

Nevertheless, departing the office empty-handed, in abject defeat, counterattack began to dominate my thoughts. She had won the first round. I had been unprepared, insufficiently armed. Consequently, I had been unceremoniously vanquished on this field of license plate–acquisition honor.

Asleep that night, an elaborate vision of revenge and retribution sprang from the depths of my primitive psyche. A strategic antidote to the day's indifferent bureaucratic injustice materialized. The opening encounter had been all hers. Tomorrow would belong to me. Payback would be a bitch. The plot sickened.

Early the next morning, I was back at the DMV office fully "armed." Some might say it was overkill, but I think not.

When you are preparing for something tantamount to mortal combat, you can't overlook anything, and I had not.

I now had in my arsenal the following "weapons": my Texas driver's license, my Texas automobile registration certificate, documentation of my insurance coverage, passport, New York birth certificate, Social Security card, Taos library card, Selective Service registration card, blood-donor card, six months' worth of Taos bank statements, an equivalent set of Taos utility statements, the day's mail, my not-yet-balanced checkbook register, a novel that I was in the midst of reading, the daily newspaper, and some trail mix.

The expected pain was to be as excruciating as it was to be prolonged. This time, though, it would be her pain; and I took perverse, sadistic, passive-aggressive pleasure anticipating every last bit of it.

She could immediately sense that I indeed had in my possession more than sufficient documentation, unequivocally entitling me to the cherished prize of New Mexico plates. Not so fast! Today was not really about license plates. It was about settling scores. Now she merely wanted to collect my money, dispense my plates, and be done with me. I, however, had other plans. Today was to be all about revenge. Today was mine. She was mine.

And so another slow-motion process unfolded, this time under my control and direction. We began with the question of documentation. I say "we," since the thrust of my strategy was to force this woman into a protracted relationship with me that she neither sought nor desired.

While she now wanted to be rid of me, I would have none of it. With her protective work counter overflowing with a veritable cornucopia of my papers and documents, I continually insisted that she and I now scrupulously examine each and every piece of paper, lest some disqualifying inconsistency be discovered.

"This is good enough," she said.

"But, let's take a look at this next one. Let's make sure. It may contain something different," was my repetitive refrain. And so it went, on and on and on, as she became hopelessly ensnared in my orchestrated drama of retribution and retaliation.

She was beginning to feel the pain. She was being forced into dialogue with me. I was reaching the soft underbelly of her vulnerability. Of this, I felt certain. I could smell blood.

Next came the ploy of the I.D. photo review and critique. I eagerly proffered my Texas driver's license. "You must have seen thousands of these photos. What do you think of this one on my Texas license? My wife says it's awful. What do you think?"

She opted for noncommittal.

"Here's my passport picture. Better or worse than the Texas license? What do you think? My wife doesn't really like that one either. She says I should try to smile more."

Stony, impatient silence.

Then came her pathetic counterpunch. "I've got to go check on something with my supervisor," she said, telegraphing a transparent facsimile of the used-car salesman's predictable tactic for gaining psychological advantage.

"No problem. Take your time. I'll just go through some of this other stuff," I replied, as I withdrew the novel and the newspaper from my holster-like briefcase. I sensed it beginning to dawn on her that her bureaucratic fortress was indeed under siege. This barbarian was at the gates!

She returned to find me wallowing like a pig in slop in the mountain of paper I had assembled. She then offered the white flag of surrender. "I've got to inspect your car. Where is it parked?" This was her obvious bid to change the momentum of the game.

"It's parked right out in front of the office," I said, in full confidence that I had a strategic counter to her ploy.

As we approached my 2002 Toyota Highlander, about which her exclusive concerns were recording the automobile's VIN and odometer reading, I struck again.

"It has over 200,000 miles on it. I think I ought to get a new one. My wife and my mechanic think it's still got a lot of life left in it. What do you think? You've probably inspected all sorts of cars."

More stony silence on her part seemed to be signaling her impending defeat. This dance of doom is approaching a crescendo. I am thrusting and she is parrying. I'm ensnaring; she's avoiding. Her mounting discomfort is increasingly evident in her curt replies. She knows that she's on the ropes, though total victory has not yet been achieved.

The final scene, a virtual coup de grace, was a matter of complete serendipity. I didn't actually know in advance that the new high-tech, security-mandated driver's license photo equipment requires that the subject not blink when the photo is being taken.

The first blink-disqualified photo was either a matter of pure accident or an instance of divine intervention. The gods probably have more on their plate than the minor details of my perverse scheme, however. So, in the absence of a clear sign from above, I'm opting for the "accident" explanation.

The next half dozen blink-corrupted photos were, however, a matter of conscious choice on my part. She would position me before the camera, urge me to hold still, activate the camera, and I would blink. She would admonish me to refrain from blinking. I would be profusely apologetic. I would vow to do better. I would then proceed to ruin the next shot in the very same way. And so it went until even I had tired of the ritual, and a blink-free photo was produced.

Finally, enough was enough. This was not, after all a monumental chess match between Bobby Fisher and Boris Spassky. I didn't really want to totally crush or destroy my adversary.

As I left the office, brand-new license plate under my arm and a temporary driver's license in my pocket, all I could think was "mission accomplished!" The forces of truth, justice, and the American way had prevailed. Payback had, indeed, been a bitch.

"...and a child shall lead them"

The Biblical words "...and a child shall lead them" have always resonated with me. Nevertheless, I don't know that I ever really took them literally. Imagine my surprise, then, finding myself doing the unthinkable: being led, both figuratively and literally, by a group of remarkable little children.

October 6, 2010, marked "Walk and Roll to School Day" in Taos. It was the local version of a national effort to encourage non-motorized school travel. Scores of area schoolchildren had assembled in Taos's Kit Carson Park on a crisp, sunny early-autumn New Mexico morning to walk and bicycle to school.

It was a magnificent sight. Shortly after sunrise, a small army of youngsters, enthusiastic, precious, and vulnerable, began trickling into the park. Their ranks steadily swelled, as departure time neared. The glow from their bright little faces magnified the day's natural sunshine. They were of a variety of adorable shapes, sizes, and shades, some toting impressive backpacks, some with tricked-out little bikes. I could barely suppress the impulse to scoop them up in my arms.

Observing the gathering throng, I recalled my own daily childhood walks to and from school. This was a glorious time.

An earlier version of this essay appeared in the Op-Ed pages of *The Taos News* on November 4, 2010.

My friends and I were together, temporarily free to joke, banter, tease, chase, and speak as we pleased. Soon, we knew we would reach the confines of the school building and be subject to its constraints…until we were once again dismissed from class for the day. Then, the cycle would reverse itself. We would be on our homeward trek, free again to walk and run and play as we chose.

As I watched this gathering of energetic and hopeful kids in the park, I became increasingly conscious of the things that I unintentionally may do that put our kids' health, safety, and well-being at risk. I'm referring to my driving.

Although I'm quick to criticize the bad driving of others, being utterly honest about it, I probably don't always exercise the care and caution that the safety of our children warrants. Sometimes I may be in too much of a hurry and exceed posted speed limits. At other times I might unthinkingly sort of roll through stop signs. Or I might reflexively increase my speed as a traffic light is cycling from green to red. Then there are the times that I inadvertently drive precariously close to a pedestrian or bicyclist.

Since I am a bit oppositional, I know in my heart that if one of these children were to call me out on my own episodically sloppy driving, I would cling fiercely to my right to drive like this. I hate being badgered, hectored, scolded, or lectured. That would probably only intensify my resistance.

To my surprise, observing these kids in their defenseless exuberance had a strong impact on me. I felt compelled to clean up my act for the sake of the children. The fact that they have not actually demanded this of me makes it all the more difficult for me to refuse to do it. I am resolved to do no less.

Perhaps other inadvertently inattentive drivers will join me in this voluntary resolve to give the kids a "brake." Our children's health and safety depends on it.

A Failure to Speak

The "crime" I witnessed was a virtual cross-cultural mugging. It was committed in broad daylight and in the presence of passive onlookers. In the moment, I lacked either the courage or the presence of mind to act in defense of its victim.

As I looked on in stunned silence, a member of my "tribe" of relatively recently settled so-called "Anglo" émigrés to these northern New Mexico mountains assaulted the dignity of a member of one of Taos's indigenous groups. The distracted store clerk had committed the presumably inexcusable sin of failing to respond fully to the patron's minor request.

The irritated customer insisted that she had made her request clear to the clerk and that he had been unforgivably inattentive. Her words were like a slap in the face.

"Boy—you need to clean out your ears!"

Though I was deeply disturbed by what I saw and heard, I said nothing.

Along with thousands of others, I adore life in Taos. I am continually awed and amazed by the rich, full, and stimulating life that Taos offers. That, however, is only part of the story. Another chapter in the continuing saga is less attrac-

An earlier version of this essay appeared in the Op-Ed pages of *The Taos News* on February 7, 2013.

tive. The open-secret back story is a tale of subsurface tensions between the different cultural groups that make this valley their home.

I confess to a bit of naïveté. I'd assumed that life in Taos would afford easy opportunities for significant friendships with members of other cultural groups.

I was wrong. Our little jewel of a town actually turns out to be something of a self-segregating society. While the tendency to stick with your own kind may generally be in the natural order of things, Taos seems to take it to a remarkable level.

Cultural intermingling is rare. Some degree of inter-group antipathy may not be far beneath the surface. Disturbingly, I am slowly coming to understand that as a newcomer, some see me as an interloper and potential usurper.

My fellow Anglos complain of slights and insults that they, too, experience. Though their grievances may also be valid, pointing fingers at others won't get us anywhere.

What, then, may be the solution? Nobody is going anywhere anytime soon, neither those who have been here for generations, nor those who got here as soon as they could. Empty platitudes ("Can't we all just get along?") are of dubious value. Ultimately, like it or not, we find ourselves in the same little lifeboat, struggling to stay afloat while seeking a way for oil and water to mix.

Yet, despite diversity-driven binds and grinds, our deeper human bond ultimately transcends our tribal differences. In critical situations, we regularly put difference aside and rush to aid and protect one another. Cultural allegiances notwithstanding, first responders automatically aid all who are in peril. More mundanely, as strangers of varied backgrounds approach one another in automobiles on our roadways, we reflexively depend on our shared humanity and reciprocal responsibilities for our very survival.

It is always easier for me to recognize the transgressions of others. However, I know that I must begin with awareness of my own failings, starting with failing to call out offending members of my own group. Perhaps those who came long before us relative newcomers will choose to do the same.

As an individual, I may not be able to do much to mitigate our tribal differences. But I can strive to better understand and respect the traditions and sensibilities of my neighbors. I can resolve to call out members of my own "family" when they are disrespectful of my neighbors' values and customs. In the grocery store on that heartbreaking day, I wish that I'd done that. I still feel ashamed that I failed to speak out.

A Persistent Pain in the Ass

It's called Parkinson's disease and I've got it. It's a neuromuscular movement disorder caused by a deficiency in dopamine, a neurotransmitter that biochemically links brain and body. Though it was diagnosed some six years ago, I've likely had it for some time. It makes movement slow, clumsy, and uncoordinated. It is a progressive, degenerative disease. There is no cure. Drug therapies moderate the symptoms, up to a point and for a time. My situation is not life threatening. It is more like a persistent pain in the ass.

Mine has been a good, full, rich "ride." I will vigorously play the hand that I've been dealt. I don't want people to feel sorry for me. I don't need their sympathy. I would be outraged by patronizing expressions of pity. And I simply will not indulge any "there but for the grace of whomever go I" guilt feelings.

Human bodies appear to have a kind of shelf life. Perhaps someone told me this on the way in, and I just wasn't listening. In any event, in my 71st year, it's a continuing challenge, living a life of my choice, as opposed to one that has been pressed upon me.

In my age cohort, everybody has something. Some struggle with acutely life-threatening conditions. Mine is not one of them. It's mostly a relentless annoyance, constantly with me, forcing its way into my consciousness, distorting and coloring my every move. Perhaps I should say "intended move," since I can't reliably make my body do what I wish it to do. My body is like a recalcitrant child, dragging its feet in opposition to a parental demand.

Regular medical consultations and efforts to force humor onto a grim circumstance are features of my existence. To my good fortune, I receive excellent medical care. My neurologist, Dr. Jill, is a recognized expert in this disease. As noted earlier, she also happens to be some six feet tall, in superb physical condition, and a martial arts competitor. My overt response to her directives is, "Yes ma'am." She urges me to get more aerobic exercise. Were I not to comply, my wife, Dianne, would rat me out in a heartbeat.

Dianne is a self-appointed one-woman truth squad. She accompanies me on my visits with Dr. Jill, lest I fail to fully and accurately report some critical aspect of my current medical status in response to the doctor's probing questions. The most recent exam eventually touched on the question of a drug's possible side effect: compulsive behaviors.

Dr. Jill inquires whether I have noticed such behavior.

"Not other than eating too much," I respond.

Detecting Dr. Jill's confirmation-seeking glance, Dianne dissents. "He's compulsively spending money…buying things."

Jill appears concerned, "Is it serious, like driving you toward bankruptcy?"

"Well, no," says Dianne.

Jill turns to me. "Exactly what are you spending money on?"

"Rubber duckies," I reply. "I've bought a few dozen of them."

I say no more. I've been "outed" in my playful acquisition and distribution of these smile-commanding bath toys. Some were gifts to my writing-class members, then in the midst of reading Donovan Hahn's *Moby Duck*.

"And how much do these rubber duckies cost?" asks my renowned neurologist.

"About a buck each," I say.

Dr. Jill has done her medical due diligence. "Look, folks, I'm a neurologist. I don't do marriage counseling. You'll just have to work this one out on your own."

And so it goes. I've always contended that a sense of humor is a distinct asset, and I'm determined to keep mine intact. Parkinson's is not a laughing matter. Many in my exclusive little club struggle mightily, as may I. Nevertheless, finding the humor in it helps ease its intrusive annoyance.

A salsa dance episode offers an example. Surprising as it may be, given my now-characteristic clumsiness, dancing is physically therapeutic. So at the behest of the "deputy exercise Nazi" with whom I live, we go to a local club for a salsa lesson.

Brief instruction period over, I am paired with a younger woman dance partner. We enter into uncertain dance embrace. Who is this woman? How will she receive my erratic touch? Can I follow the dance instruction just received? Will my efforts satisfy and please this stranger?

My right arm is around my new partner. My left arm is raised, gently taking her compliant right hand. We begin to move with the Latin rhythms spun by the club DJ. As if on cue, my elevated hand begins to tremble. A mild parkinsonian tremor has suddenly surfaced. My shaking hand puzzles, distracts, and confuses my partner. She is unaware that it is a symptom of a disease. "Who are you waving at?" she innocently inquires. I suppress my laughter.

People with Parkinson's disease seem reflexively to withdraw from athletic recreation. Contrarian that I am, I do not. Instead, I have adopted a philosophy that I call "adaptive denial." It is shorthand for my refusal to forsake significant aspects of my life until I see incontrovertible evidence that I must.

Skiing had become something of an unsettling challenge, but given my adaptive-denial philosophy, I refused to hang it up. I theorized that with better equipment and good instruction, I would triumph over my physical limitations. My breakthrough solution was Taos Ski Valley's vaunted "Ski Week": a high-quality ski lesson every morning for an entire week. This, I imagined, would surely compensate for my physical limitations.

Ski Week arrives, and I am on the mountain for "ski off." Students are poised to ski a stretch of the mountain, demonstrating their skills before the group of observing instructors.

Anxiety builds as I await my turn. Finally, with adrenaline flowing, I shoot down the mountain, past the arrayed instructors, make a single turn, and stop. The ski-school head concludes from this exhibition that I am an exceptionally aggressive skier and assigns me to a class level far above what I know my skill level to be.

"Class 7," he announces.

On the verge of panic, I picture myself thrust into extreme, death-defying ski challenges.

"I appreciate the compliment, but with all due respect, that is a level far above where I belong," I tell him.

The instructor is irritated. "I've done this for many years, with hundreds of students. I know where you belong."

Following a protracted, animated mountainside debate, I make a last ditch effort to save myself from impending orthopedic surgery. I spill the beans.

"You were not seeing what you think you were seeing. I'm not an aggressive skier. I've got a neurological disorder. You were watching a man 'shopping' for a turn."

He finally hears my plea and demotes me to "class 3." I live to ski another day.

Humor aside, visions of my endgame are never far from my thoughts. Though I am neither clinically depressed nor suicidal, I know that eventually my time will have passed. It will be time to go. On an occupational level, I fear that I will be slow in recognizing when that time has come. I dread the thought that an errant tremor might be misinterpreted as anxiety or uncertainty, compromising my professional credibility.

Dignity, if not humor, demands the judgment and the means to recognize and to act when I have reached the end of my very good ride. I sometimes fantasize having a grand celebratory farewell party just prior to bringing down the final curtain on my personal play's good run. Seeking the "Goldilocks" moment (not too early, not too late, but just right), timing will likely be everything.

Quest for the Cure

Parkinson's disease reminds me of the lyrics of an old song. "Every step you take, every move you make, I'll be watching you." No matter the circumstance, there it is, slowing me down, coloring and distorting my every movement. Now, even my friends were watching me.

Jim and Virginia were both convinced that a visitor from the Far East had a cure for my disease. Each had separately telephoned me, urging me to attend a rare local presentation by a famous Traditional Chinese Medicine (TCM) healer. I was so moved by my friends' concern that, despite my skepticism, I agreed to attend.

The next evening, Dianne and I made our way through falling snow to Taos's Willow Clinic. The afflicted had come, like pilgrims to Lourdes, seeking the equivalent of holy waters to cure our disabling affliction.

Doctor Huo was to share the "good news" of the curative powers of acupuncture with the people of Taos. Fresh from his self-trumpeted worldwide tour, Huo had traveled from Shanghai, China, and Orlando/Winter Park, Florida, to introduce the vast curative powers of acupuncture to those suffering from Parkinson's disease.

There we sat, some two dozen of the afflicted and those who love and care for us, packed into a haphazardly furnished reception area. We were surrounded by shelves of large glass jars filled with exotic-looking herbal remedies. A rag-tag collection of chairs, repeatedly rearranged to accommodate the trickle of late arrivals, pointed toward a desk at the front of the room on which a small video monitor was precariously perched.

Scanning the growing crowd, I recognized several friends, fellow members of my exclusive little "club." Were they any more optimistic than I? If so, I pitied these poor, naïve souls.

Doctor Huo — a jovial, high-energy, Chinese-accented speaker — opened the program with a half-hour introduction to the TCM theory underpinning acupuncture (yin-yang, chi-blood, and so on). The language and concepts felt strange to me. Nevertheless, I was committed to hearing the man out.

The program unfolded with two hours of video clips. First was a series of archival Florida TV news reports on the medical miracles performed by Huo himself. Then came multiple breathless, enthusiastic patient testimonials demonstrating Huo's astounding cures for a virtually limitless range of medical conditions. Indeed, he claimed to cure almost anything.

Doctor Huo, now gonzo journalist, held center stage with videotaped cures of patient after patient, all interviewed in *cinéma vérité* style. Patient interviews were punctuated by Huo's self-congratulatory, interjection: "Wow!" In Dr. Huo's hands, acupuncture was apparently nothing short of a miracle cure.

Video testimonials were interspersed with the doctor's declarations of his medical and physical prowess, his international reputation, photographic documentation of his qi gong expertise, and a certificate confirming his international "Who's Who" listing. He seemed a legend in his own mind. What a guy! Right here, in tiny, isolated Taos, New Mexico.

Finally, I could no longer contain myself. My skepticism got the best of me. The question that I had been stifling for hours broke through, disrupting the rapt attention of the assembly.

"Doctor Huo," I began, "will you be taking questions?"

"Yes, of course," was his enthusiastic reply.

My monologue began. "With all due respect (disrespectful comments are always preceded by that phrase), this is an audience of vulnerable and impressionable people. Anecdotes and testimonials can get us only so far. We'd all like a miracle. But my experience is that when something seems to be too good to be true, it generally is. I am a product of Western scientific thought. Can you point us toward some research supporting the effectiveness of these treatments?"

Doctor Huo appeared puzzled. He responded with his assertion of a personal "85 percent success rate."

"No, that's not what I'm asking. I'm interested in empirical data, randomized clinical trials, double-blind studies."

Doctor Huo appeared even more bewildered. Then, his handlers stepped in with efforts to translate the gist of my query. This impromptu mini-briefing did not seem to be taking hold. Doctor Huo continued to look befuddled.

Finally, I volunteered another comment. "I looked at a review of the research this morning. The authors' conclusion was that data are 'not convincing'."

The alternative medicine devotees immediately sprang to TCM's defense, reacting as if I were some Western-medical establishment agent provocateur. Both the clinic's visibly uncomfortable owner and a visiting acupuncturist declared Western scientific method irrelevant to the truths of TCM, which, they lectured, had been practiced for 5,000 years. "Narrow, limited methodology," was their summary judgment of Western medical science.

Now slowly shuffling toward the exit, the audience wordlessly signaled the gathering's adjournment. Had I torpedoed the meeting?

It was a dilemma for me and for my struggling cohort. Who knows what promise this ancient wisdom might hold? I couldn't tell from the presentation's hype. It fed my skepticism and my yearning.

By Western standards, the evidence may not be there. Nevertheless, this alternative medical approach might have value. It was hard to know, given Doctor Huo's effort to indoctrinate and persuade.

Do we follow our hearts or our heads? We, with this disease, know that as far as the ability to control our bodies' movements goes, our heads are not really doing so well. Perhaps our hearts will do better. The potential downside would be yet another dashed hope, another broken heart.

What's a Parkinson's patient to do? Perhaps, in the end, we suspend disbelief, follow our dreams, and give it a try.

A Virtual Ménage à Trois

Although I love living in Taos, every so often I just need to get out of town. These trips include a regular companion who, in the interests of marital harmony, I refer to simply as "Jane." From Dianne's reaction to Jane, you'd think I had unilaterally transformed our marriage into a ménage à trois. I just don't understand why Dianne doesn't seem to trust me with her.

On a recent road trip to the Oregon coast, I sensed some antipathy on Dianne's part toward Jane: "Do you really need her? Can't you shut her up? She is so annoying. I don't like the sound of her voice."

I should probably feel embarrassed to admit it: Though my relationship with Jane is basically one of convenience, I am totally infatuated with her.

Jane is my travel companion and navigator, but she is not my copilot. That would be Dianne, the love of my life. My travels with Jane are strictly business.

I do not have sexual fantasies about Jane. Well, maybe I've had just one or two. It's not that I don't have thoughts about her when she's not with me. I do. I imagine her angular features, her compact body, and her stylish, businesslike appearance.

An earlier version of this essay appeared in *Chokecherries,* May 2011.

I am enthralled with Jane. A lot of it is her British accent, the calm, clipped, clear enunciation that is the delightful sound of her voice. I've always been a sucker for women with sophisticated foreign accents. Hearing that sound, I instantly assume that she absolutely knows whereof she speaks. Her voice is music to my ears. I am immediately under her spell.

Jane does not mince words. She silently tracks my driving, and when absolutely necessary, pipes up with a bit of sage advice: "Left turn ahead — right turn — turn around when possible — take the left lane — in 300 yards stay right — you have reached your destination." Her word choices sometimes surprise me. She may urge me to "take the motorway" or to keep "straight on."

Jane is petite. Her tiny size may even be part of her attraction. She is small enough for me to simply whisk her off with me. Flat chested though she may be, she is one hell of a little package.

Jane is always "locked and loaded." There is no waiting around for her to find her purse, her sunglasses, her book, her cell phone, or her keys. She is the lowest-maintenance woman I have ever known.

Vacationing with Dianne on the breathtaking and jaw-dropping Oregon coast was a dream come true. I assumed, naïvely perhaps, that having Jane along would merely help us find our way amid the spectacular scenery. What's all the fuss?

My former wife, not one of my big fans, used to tell me, somewhat snidely, that what I was seeking in life was a totally liberated woman who would do precisely as I commanded her to do.

Is there a problem with that? From my ex's lips to God's ear, Jane is that woman. She is the girl of my dreams. My wish is her command. There is no drama with her, just total obedience to my direction. It sounds almost too good to be true.

Prior to Jane, I never once paid for the "services" of a woman. However, given her looks and skill, I consider her the bargain of the century. I'm not being at all immodest when I say that I can get Jane turned on almost instantly. All I have to do is to touch her in just the right places. I'm not bragging. Nor am I some kind of Don Juan. She has matter-of-factly let me know exactly where to touch her to get her to satisfy my needs. She's easy.

When we are on the road together, Jane keeps a focused, watchful eye on our route. She never naps or has a lapse in attention, not even for an instant. "Reliable" must be her middle name.

I have no illusions about Jane's capacity for loyalty. She would go home with another man in a flash. All he would have to do is pick her up and carry her off. I have learned to live with this.

Jane is not the least bit coy. She is totally out there on display. You can read her like a virtual book. She makes her opinions crystal clear. Yet, she never badgers or scolds me when I don't heed her advice. If I miss a turn, she is simply likely to say, "Turn around when possible." I guess she could say "please."

Jane has incredible discipline. She speaks only when necessary. In fact, I have known her to remain silent for more than a hundred miles, breaking her silence at the precise moment her intervention is required.

Never before have I met a woman who was content with such total lack of attention. I actually ignore Jane for long periods. Yet she never insists that we have "the conversation," the one that begins something like, "Just what are we to each other?"

Other women in my life have been quite willing to tell me "where to get off." They, however, were critical or rejecting. Jane never expresses any sense of disapproval. She inevitably conveys the feeling that she has my best interests at heart and that my goals would be better served by some course correction. She must be among the most gentle of critics.

Even when Jane is monitoring my speed, she never utters a scolding, "Slow down!" That simply would not fit with her supportive demeanor. She plainly lets me know how fast I'm going and she silently turns a little bit red in registering her concern. That's my "gentle Jane."

Lately I've noticed that Jane is beginning to grow on Dianne. I would never dare say this to her, but I sense her budding curiosity regarding Jane's opinions.

As we drive across the badlands of the Southwest, I see Dianne out of the corner of my eye surreptitiously checking to see what Jane estimates as our time of arrival. In an unguarded moment, Dianne will even ask me what Jane thinks about our preferred route of travel.

Could there be more than a developing connection between my dual (or perhaps dueling) female travel companions? Who would have thought it? It will take all the discipline I can muster to forbear pointing out this apparent relationship breakthrough. I am struggling to suppress a smug smile.

Just drive. Pretend not to notice anything out of the ordinary. Stifle the urge to say, "It looks like you're becoming just a wee bit fond of Jane." Do not gloat.

My chest swells with pride. Not merely one but two females in my life are dedicated to helping me make my way in an unfamiliar world. I am doubly blessed.

I will follow Jane's advice most anywhere. In life, you take your guidance and your driving directions wherever you find them.

I wonder how things would work out on a European adventure with both Jane and Dianne. On second thought, that might just be a bridge too far.

American Politics

The Things They Came With

They came with dreams and they came with nightmares. They came with words of fairness and they came with talk of justice. They came in search of truth and they came with little power. They came with independence and they came with growing courage.

They came with signs and they came with slogans. They came with cell phones and they came with iPads. They came with Facebook and they came with Twitter. They came with voices and they came with visions. They came with tents and they came with books. They came with "bat signal" and they came with "mic check."

They came with marches and they came with sit-ins. They came with manifestos and they came with dialogues. They came with songs and they came with speeches. They came with chants and they came with choruses. They came with irreverence and they came with improvisation.

They came with youth and they came with hope. They came with the many and they came with the peaceful. They came with the young and they came with the old. They came with their brothers and they came with their sisters. They

---

Earlier versions of this essay appeared in the Op-Ed pages of *The Taos News* on December 15, 2011, and in *HOWL: The Voice of UNM–Taos*, Spring 2012.

came with Martin and they came with Abraham. They came with Bobby and they came with John.

They came with torment and they came with anguish. They came with illness and they came with hunger. They came with sunshine and they came with storm. They came with communion and they came with diversity. They came with tactic and they came with principle. They came with yearning and they came with disappointment. They came forlorn and they came discarded. They came with shroud and they came with spotlight. They came with facts and they came with feelings. They came with purpose and they came with commitment.

They came without rancor and they came not for retribution. They came in rising numbers and they came in mounting forces. They came under criticism and they came with derision. They came with pleadings and they came with questions. They came with innocence and they came with idealism. They came with human bodies and they came with abstract concepts. They came with broken bones and they came with brutal bruises.

They came with insight and they came with prescience. They came in quest and they came in conclave. They came in witness and they came in warning.

Surrogate others also came. They came with orders and they came with mission. They came with the darkness and came with the daylight. They came in black and they came in blue. They came with "intelligence" and they came with stupidity.

They came with protection and they came with barricades. They came with horses and they came with armor. They came with helmets and they came with face masks.

They came with pepper spray and they came with tear gas. They came with bullets and they came with "batons." They came with squads and they came with armies.

They came with fear and they came with fury. They came with denial and they came with ridicule. They came with disdain and they came with denigration. They came with power and they came with terror. They came with chaos and they came with confusion. They came with weapons and they came with combat.

They came without warmth and they came without feeling. They came without pity and they came without mercy. They came without compassion and they came without generosity. They came without kindness and they came without understanding. They came without sympathy and they came without decency.

They came as demanded and they came as directed. They came with command and they came with control. They came in assigned roles and they came as required. They came with split loyalty and they came with hard hearts.

They came with judgment and they came with punishment. They came with guilt and they came with shame.

The occupiers came yet again. They came with our dormant dreams and they came with our heavy hearts. They came in suffering and they came in sacrifice. They came in our interests and they came for our welfare. They came in our place and they came in our stead. They came with the 99 percent and they came with us.

For the Soul of a Nation

I was stunned by a 2009 *Christian Science Monitor* news item. Alarmingly, some Christian "conservatives" had been invoking verses from Psalm 109 in their prayers for President Obama: "Let his days be few; and let another take his place. Let his children be fatherless, and his wife be a widow. Let his children be wandering beggars" (109:8–9).

Free speech notwithstanding, how could anyone not be horrified by this? What have we come to as a people if this is the font of presumably religious people's prayers?

It is tempting to dismiss such a prayer as the ranting of the deeply misguided. It may indeed be that. Much more ominous, however, is the likelihood that this "prayer" is a symptom of a deeper and far more troubling problem, one that goes to the heart of who we as a nation have become.

I, too, fear for our nation. However, I believe that the real threat comes not from our elected president but rather in the form of the epic struggle in which we are now embroiled.

It is a battle for no less than our collective American soul: who we are, aspire to be, and will become. It is fundamentally a struggle between two competing belief systems

An earlier version of this essay appeared in the Op-Ed pages of *The Taos News* on December 3, 2009.

or "religions": one that asserts a shared moral imperative to care for the weak, the vulnerable, the oppressed, and the sick among us; and the other that does not accept such a collective obligation. Wouldn't Jesus have almost certainly taken the former path? It's quite unlikely that the major national political players are reliable allies in this struggle. Deplorably, we have the best government that money can buy.

The effort to effect large-scale health-care legislative reform is a concrete political example of this divide. Those on the Right deride enactment of Affordable Healthcare legislation as "Obamacare." They characterize it as tantamount to socialism, and mount repeated efforts to overturn it. But, aren't one's health and life a fundamental civil right? Our fellow Americans would suffer and die without the increased access to medical care that this legislation brings. Isn't a humane society obliged to care for its most vulnerable members?

On a personal level, I value and respect my friends whose political affiliations I do not share. Some are among the most generous people I have ever known.

On a national level, however, it's quite another matter. There we have a shameless Republican Party, seemingly devoid of human decency, compassion, honor, or integrity.

And then there are the Democrats: often lacking in political courage, they are the hapless perennial Charlie Browns of politics, watching helplessly as their football is stolen again and again and again. What a dismal choice of saviors.

Where does this leave those of us who fear for the very soul of our nation? It is highly unlikely that we can persuade those who offer horrific prayers for our president that they are misguided. Since people cannot be talked out of fixed, firm, non-rational beliefs, our energies are far better spent in efforts to understand and to address the deep terrors that drive our fellow citizens to offer appalling prayers for our president. Could anything other than fear explain their behavior?

They, too, are our brothers, sisters, friends, and neighbors. Their fears must be our fears and must be of abiding concern for us all. Though the means to achieve this are unclear, we must somehow assure our disaffected brothers and sisters that we are as committed to *their* protection from the demons that terrorize them as we are to our own.

Feelings, Faith, and Facts

The whole thing is driving me a little nuts. I used to joke that I was sometimes uninformed, yet never in doubt. The joke has become the new reality. Uninformed, fact-free political and policy positions are now all the rage. The current norm seems to be, "Don't confuse me with the facts. I already have my mind made up." Facts no longer appear to matter.

Daniel Patrick Moynihan's words remain dear to my heart: "Everyone is entitled to his own opinion, but not his own facts." Now, when credibility is accorded anyone with a media megaphone, Moynihan's declaration seems quaint.

The debate concerning global climate change is a case in point. The weight of scientific opinion yields an overwhelming consensus judgment. Nevertheless, climate change deniers persist in citing outlying and often tainted findings as if there really is a serious counterargument.

Our Texas neighbors insist that history textbooks be rewritten to represent so-called "facts" conforming to their particular extreme ideological positions. Locally, we see challenges to the theory of evolution based on its critics' deep religious faith. On a national level, a segment of the population is certain that President Obama, despite his professed Christianity, is a closet Muslim. These critical souls apparently possess some divinely inspired secret insight into other people's theological thoughts.

Perhaps this is the inevitable legacy of the "faith-based" political ideology of the Bush era. George W. Bush's administration held it to be a slam-dunk certainty that weapons of mass destruction would be found in Iraq. If a nation can go to war based on gut feelings, not facts, is there any conceivable national policy that would be off limits to feeling-based justification?

It's as if there's an ongoing struggle between our nation's fact constituency and its faith constituency. People will inevitably cling to their beliefs no matter what the facts.

Dramatic examples of this all-too-human phenomenon are present in the belief systems of so-called "doomsday" cults. Despite unequivocal predictions of the end of the world, a date certain arrives and the sun rises, birds sing, and human beings go about the business of living. Nevertheless, cult members never concede that their prophesies were wrong.

Republican doomsayers had similar sky-is-falling predictions regarding the consequences of enacting Obamacare: government "death panels" would "pull the plug on Grandma," socialized medicine, the end of freedom and democracy as we know it. Somehow I doubt we will ever hear them say, "We were wrong."

News outlets compound the facts-versus-feelings problem in concluding that there are always multiple meritorious points of view. Taken to its extreme, this stance would imply that to be truly "fair and balanced," a news story on the Holocaust would deserve a response by a Nazi apologist.

In this zeitgeist, the uncritical verdict of the *Alice in Wonderland* dodo prevails. "All have won and each must have a prize." Feelings are as good as facts. It is as if George Orwell's 1984 had arrived. Good is bad, black is white, truth is fiction, facts are falsehoods, and feelings are tantamount to facts.

One longs for an earlier age, in which Senator Moynihan's words enjoyed routine acceptance and even reverence. Heretofore, knowledge always trumped ignorance. We may now have reached a point where emotion trumps reason.

The countless good works of people of faith merit enormous respect and admiration. Most believers may even be convinced that the facts are on their side. On the other hand, they may have taken to heart an assertion variously attributed to both Mark Twain and Benjamin Disraeli: "There are lies, damn lies, and statistics."

Since reason seems to no longer carry the day, many now depend on the political wisdom of comedians such as Jon Stewart ("Rally to Restore Sanity") and Stephen Colbert ("March to Keep Fear Alive") to bring us to our senses. What must that say about the state of our body politic?

The whole thing makes my head swim. Perhaps the best we can hope for from the fact-challenged, freewheeling forces of unmodulated feeling are the words of the late Gilda Radner's famous "Saturday Night Live" character Emily Litella: "Never mind."

When Prophesy Fails

Many of my friends on the Right were clearly stunned by the outcome of our 2012 presidential election. President Obama and the Democratic Party won broad and resounding electoral victories. For many Republicans, this was a shocker. *What happened?*

Despite potential access to reliable, objective data accurately predicting the Election Day outcome, the Republican Party, its presidential candidate, its opinion leaders, and its so-called "news" organizations were totally flummoxed by the election results. They didn't see the equivalent of electoral annihilation coming.

How could Republicans have been so blind? How could they have been caught so off guard? How could they have been so unaware of the impending electoral tsunami hiding in plain sight? How could their predictions have been so spectacularly wrong?

There is a long history of so-called "conservative" Republican skirmishes with facts. Republican ideologues are found in the forefront of fact-challenged causes: global climate-change denial, rejection of natural selection/evolution theory, and "birther" challenges to the legitimacy of our president, to name a few. With this anti-intellectual culture as prelude, could it be a genuine surprise that Republicans favored feelings over facts when it came to understanding where they actually stood in the run-up to the recent electoral contest?

Clinging to beliefs in the face of facts is not unique to today's Republicans. Indeed, Republican insistence on ideological purity and obedience to dogma and doctrine in the face of clear, objective data to the contrary finds a compelling parallel in the behavior of so-called "doomsday" cults that prophesy the end of the world.

And so it is with today's Republicans. They isolate themselves in echo-chamber bubbles in which they are repeatedly told just what they want to hear. And now, in the wake of their resounding defeat at the polls, any explanation will do, save one that concludes, "We were wrong—wrong on policy, wrong on program, wrong on candidates, wrong on message, wrong on strategy, wrong on commitment to feelings over facts, wrong, wrong, wrong."

The Republicans' fact-free chickens have come home to roost. The pervasive Republican culture of denial in the face of compelling contrary data has hoisted that party on its own petard. In the end, ideology does not trump knowledge, and knowledge inevitably does trump ignorance.

As the Bible says, "Ye shall know the truth, and the truth shall make you free." Despite a foreboding sense that some things may be too terrible to know, little comfort is ever achieved by killing off a truth-bearing messenger.

Our best governance requires the participation of a rational, loyal opposition. We are all better off when our electoral contests are between sane, loyal opponents. Listen well, Republicans. The sound you may hear is the voice of the voters.

Taking Our Country Back

President Obama has acted in ways that reinforce some Republicans' beliefs that he is not a true American and that we must take our country back. Take the killing of Osama bin Laden, for example. A genuine American would have given bin Laden a running head start, just like we used to do as kids playing hide and seek. "W" had no problem doing that at Tora Bora. You don't simply track down a mass murderer, corner him, and kill him. You are supposed to engineer a suspense-building opportunity for him to slip through your fingers. Isn't that how they do it in the movies? You keep the audience constantly scared out of their wits and primed for the sequel. How could someone actually born in the USA, home to the Hollywood movie industry, be so ignorant of basic theatrics?

Growing up in Hawaii or Indonesia or wherever he was really born, Obama sure did not learn much about manners. Take his response to the Republican fiscal austerity plan. Obama made a speech about *his* deficit reduction plan and invited Republicans to sit right in the front row. He had the gall to disagree with them publicly, and wound up hurting their feelings. Didn't he know that you do not disagree with people right to their faces? You always do that behind their backs.

An earlier version of this essay appeared in the Op-Ed pages of *The Taos News* on June 16, 2011.

Think about those poor Republicans, stuck there with Obama looking them right in the eye and straight-out telling them that their plan is costly, callous, misguided, and wrong. Talk about a sucker punch! That's what secret backroom negotiations are for. Republicans thought they could count on this guy. He had been their patsy for how long now? He's just like that nerdy fraternity brother who always insisted that the college honor code was worth something more than the paper it was printed on. What a dork!

Republicans clearly thought they had an understanding with Obama: they play offense, he plays defense; they throw the punches, and he does the "rope-a-dope"; they say anything they darn well please, and he tries to find some negotiating room in it. Just where does he get off changing the rules and pulling this sneak attack on them? Blitzkrieg was supposed to be theirs. How does he get to ambush them like that?

Some people think that Republicans don't have feelings. I know for a fact that they most certainly do have feelings — just not for poor people, minorities, union workers, public employees, and all those people who have not pulled themselves up by their family bootstraps. Isn't that what families are for? They help you to get into a good college, buy a house, start a business, and get another shot at success when the first one or two or three or more fail.

It's so refreshing to see Republicans put their political muscle and money behind their ideology. So what if public opinion is against them when it comes to their policies regarding changing Social Security and Medicare? Republicans know better about these things than ordinary people do. They get regular advice from financial industry experts. Who would know better than the people actually running things?

Just what is the problem with Wall Street wanting to make money off these programs? Isn't that the American way?

I just love that Paul Ryan — so smart, articulate, Midwestern looking. What an economics stud! He sure looks like the future face of the Republican Party. What dedication and determination this guy shows. No weak-kneed, spineless wimp here. Obama talks of "shared sacrifice," but Ryan has the smarts and the guts to have offered a plan to do just that: share sacrifice among the very people who are most experienced with sacrifice: the poor, the weak, and the elderly. You really don't want rich people who have never sacrificed to be just trying it out it in the midst of a crisis.

Republicans understand that to reach deficit-reduction goals, you have to be willing to throw some people under the bus. The poor, weak, and elderly are probably a good place to start. They already have sacrifice experience. Besides, what do they really contribute to the economy anyway?

Maybe I'm a bit naïve, but I think Republicans are awesome. How could you not be impressed by their total dedication to taking our country back…waaay back? Now, that's change you can believe in!

Treason?

How could I have been so wrong? How could I have so seriously misunderstood them?

Confession is purportedly good for the soul. So let me take the plunge and confess that I may have completely misunderstood the Republican Congressional Tea Party Caucus. I had come to believe that U.S. House Republican tea-baggers had pointedly violated their sworn, sacred oath to preserve, protect, and defend the Constitution of these United States, and in so doing had acted in a manner tantamount to treason.

Naïvely, I reread Article 14 of the U.S. Constitution. It plainly states, "The validity of the public debt of the United States, authorized by law ... shall not be questioned." You can look it up. Yet, Congressional tea-baggers had mounted an all-out refusal to permit vital legislation raising the level of the national debt, opposition forbidden by the same Constitution they had pledged to serve. They had not only questioned the validity of our legally authorized public debt, but they appeared to have done everything possible to sabotage implementation of this section of the Constitution. In their fervor, they seemed willing to drive our economy off a

An earlier version of this essay appeared in the Op-Ed pages of *The Taos News* on September 22, 2011.

cliff. How could they have acted without any sense of honor or loyalty to the Constitution and to our nation? And how could I have so misjudged them?

Much to my relief, I have finally gained a degree of enlightenment in the matter. I now understand that my apparent confusion is likely related to the tea-baggers' deep religious convictions. Almost without exception, you see, they routinely declare their close connection with the Almighty. Indeed, Rick Perry and Michele Bachmann told us that God called them to run for president in 2012. It puzzled me that God commanded both of them to run, but that may be another matter. Perhaps God just enjoys a good horse race now and then.

In any event, you simply cannot ask religious zealots to choose between obedience to their God and an oath that they may have sworn to an Earthly proposition. God's will automatically transcends a promise made to a merely human enterprise, even if it is the United States Constitution. In appreciating the Tea Party Caucus's overarching duty to a higher power, what looked like treason now seems like an understandable and pardonable article of deep religious faith. I apologize for my earlier rush to judgment.

The only problem I'm still having with my new understanding is that somehow the tea-baggers' God seemed like a dead ringer for Grover Norquist, revered prophet of the fervent religious sect, Americans for Tax Reform. Congressional tea-baggers swore an inviolate oath to obey his sole commandment: "No new taxes!" Perhaps I just heard it wrong. Maybe tea-baggers were referring to Norquist as "Greed, himself" and not "God, himself." My hearing is just not as good as it used to be.

There's another part of my confusion with the tea-baggers' proclaimed religious commitment. I had always understood Jesus to have been a liberal or at least a compassionate conservative. Hadn't he preached that we should comfort the afflicted, protect the weak, feed the hungry, shelter the homeless, and so on?

Maybe Congressional tea-baggers are traitors after all — both to their Constitution and their God. On the other hand, perhaps they are merely the equivalent of Congressional class clowns, trapped in their own practical joke. I think I'm becoming confused again.

An Unrequited "Love"

It certainly felt like unrequited love. Perhaps you have finally learned your lesson. In your first presidential campaign, I voted for you, worked in your campaign, and contributed money to your cause. I also gave my heart to you, Barack. Despite the absence of any apparent fire in your belly, your eloquence, intelligence, seemingly progressive intentions, relaxed good looks, and winning smile seduced me. I swallowed your "audacity of hope" and dared to dream of something new under the sun. Silly me!

Once you had stolen my heart, what did you go and do? You immediately started flirting with the likes of Susan Collins, Olympia Snowe, and Chuck Grassley, those conniving triflers with your affections. Then, to top it all off, you got into bed with Mitch McConnell and John Boehner, of all people. It added insult to injury, cavorting with those deceivers, manipulators, and seducers, while my intentions were unquestionably pure.

I could have told you that they were only toying with you, that they would never return your affections. They were never going to give themselves over to you as I had

An earlier version of this essay appeared in the Op-Ed pages of *The Taos News* on December 30, 2010.

been prepared to do. They would only use you and shamelessly abuse you. They would offer the pretense of openness to your overtures; but they were just leading you on. It's a story as old as time, one about which parents caution their inexperienced and vulnerable offspring.

In the end, "Love hath no fury like a [voter] scorned." We previously neglected lovers are keeping you at arm's length. We longed for relationship yet remained alert to the prospect of betrayal. We were "once burned, twice shy."

"You dance with the one that brung ya." These words of legendary Texas football coach, Darrell Royal, capture our disaffection. Royal was originally talking football strategy. Yet his words reflect a pithy, intuitive understanding of human relationships. They are fundamentally about loyalty. In the end, you stick with those who stuck with you. To do otherwise inevitably invites the fury evoked by betrayal, the fierce animus of the rejected lover.

Here is where our political "love" relationship now stands. We have been estranged. Our hearts have been broken, though perhaps not irreparably. You act as if you have turned over a new leaf. Do we take you back? Do we trust again? Do we risk yet another broken heart?

Your conciliatory inclinations are admirable. You are probably hardwired by life experience to accommodate and collaborate. Nevertheless, these instincts are now totally misplaced. There is nobody on the other side with whom to find common cause. They pick your pocket, steal your lunch, and stab you in the back every time. Haven't you noticed?

Then there is the issue of being willing to fight for those and for what you profess to love. A lover worth his salt will fight to protect those dear to him. Barack, we know that you are able to take a punch. We have also seen you throw a few lately. We hope you can keep this up.

Muhammad Ali, arguably one of the greatest fighters of all time, paid a dear price for the very "rope-a-dope" tactic that you seemed determined to imitate. He absorbed his opponents' blows as his adversaries exhausted themselves throwing punch after punch at him. Sadly, all those shots to the head have caused him brain damage. We don't want that to be your fate.

Nancy Pelosi, one tough legislator and grandma, presented a better model for fighting back and refusing to "go gently into that good night," as right-wing perpetrators of the recent political big lie intended. They unconscionably damned and dishonored her for tactical political purposes. They shamelessly turned her into a caricature and a talking point, and when they were through beating her up, she was supposed to disappear. Instead of quietly slinking off, though, she refused to play the passive, vanquished victim role that the Right had scripted for her and just quietly fade away into political obscurity.

Politics is said to be the art of the possible. Nevertheless, we will need some clear and unmistakable sign that you have mended your ways and are chastened by your earlier naïveté.

We know that personal change requires courage and discipline. We wary lovers warily watch and wait.

How Dare You, Warren Buffett?

Just because you are a multibillionaire, where do you get off volunteering to have your income taxes raised? Your secretary pays income taxes at a higher rate than you do? Well, what's the problem with that? Let her look out for herself. If she's not clever enough to find some tax loophole, she deserves to pay a higher rate. Why bother us? Wall Street "masters of the universe" should enjoy some advantages over ordinary people. Besides, if you promote the idea that your taxes should be raised, people will expect the same from the rest of us super-rich.

You contend that the nation cannot solve its fiscal problems without additional revenue. That's exactly the point. We don't really want any additional revenue, no matter what the source. It's part of our plan to "starve the beast." You may live in Omaha, but wake up and smell the coffee!

You say that rich people receive disproportionate benefit from our society, and that it is only right that we pay our fair share in taxes. Perhaps you recall that your hero John F. Kennedy famously pointed out that life is inherently unfair.

An earlier version of this essay appeared in the Op-Ed pages of *The Taos News* on November 10, 2011.

People need to stop whining and just get used to it. You are not helping this. You are encouraging a dangerous fantasy of fairness. How dare you?

Just who do you think you are? You haven't fooled us with this generous, patriotic, populist pose of yours. You started out getting some pretty good publicity: "Multibillionaire wants to pay more in taxes." Well, we'll fix that. You've heard of our "Swift Boat" tactics, once used to make a war hero out to be a liar and a coward. Think what we could do to a geriatric like you.

We've had experience with traitors to their upper-class status. There was that so-called aristocrat Franklin Delano Roosevelt pushing through the whole Social Security idea. We've still got our hands full trying to undo that one. It's like some monster you just can't kill. Believe me, we've tried. The American people may love it, but we're not finished trying to gut it.

We haven't forgotten President Kennedy's betrayal of his upper-class roots, either. He flat-out said, "If a free society cannot protect the many who are poor, it cannot save the few who are rich." That sort of talk set us back 20 years. President Reagan finally got us on the right track with the idea that government is the enemy. As you well know, we've spent vast sums of money on so-called think tanks and lobbyists getting the American people to actually believe this government-as-enemy stuff.

We have been doing our best to persuade people that socialism is a grave threat to the country, except of course when it involves the government bailout of our too-big-to-fail financial institutions. Don't go getting any crazy ideas about letting people know that plutocracy is the real threat.

"Plutocracy" is such an unfamiliar word and it's better kept that way. Only those of us who can handle the cold, hard truth need to know that it means government of the rich, by the rich, and for the rich, just as it should be. Thank God the Supreme Court is on the side of plutocracy.

Look, Buffett, if you want to pay more tax, just go right ahead. Treat the U.S. Treasury like some charity or church that accepts contributions or tithes. We have no problem with that. That's our whole point. Churches and charities should take care of the poor, just as they did in 18th- and 19th-century Great Britain. Just leave the rest of us out of it. What if there isn't nearly enough charity to take care of all the problems? Haven't you ever heard of survival of the fittest?

Next, you'll be volunteering to pay more inheritance tax on all those billions, if you haven't already given it away to that Bill and Melinda Gates do-gooder foundation. Just because some of us were born on third base and act like we hit triples, that's no reason to believe that our families shouldn't accumulate more and more wealth. So what if our heirs never do anything to deserve great wealth beyond being born lucky? Who cares if transfer of wealth within our families turns our country into a banana republic?

Now, about that "class warfare" thing: just remember that we're masters of it. We've been at it for decades. Just look at what we've done to unions, workers, and the middle class.

Watch yourself, Buffett. This ain't beanbag.

A Death in the Family

There has been a devastating death in our American family. The deceased had been critically ill, beyond hope, and on life support. We have finally pulled the plug. Our American Dream has died.

As it drew its last breath, those ministering to it could hear confusion and disorientation in its whispered final words and deepening death rattle. "Why did you abandon me? You had always aimed higher and been better than this. We were family. We were each other's keeper. In the best of times and in the worst of times, we would always 'hold hands and stick together.' Where has your love for me gone?"

Heroic intervention was either unavailable or unsuccessful. The autopsy conclusion was "electrolyte imbalance." That's probably medical shorthand for the delicate equilibrium required to keep a beloved dream alive. It seems that even strongly cherished dreams need careful feeding and protection to survive. Ours had suffered unendurable neglect.

Some family members say a broken heart was the cause of death, that The Dream could no longer endure the disregard, indifference, ridicule, and hostility of estranged extend-

An earlier version of this essay appeared in the Op-Ed pages of *The Taos News* on April 28, 2011.

ed-family members, that the family feud had become deeply destructive. Those who embraced The Dream tried to reassure it that disaffected family members meant well, that it was simply a misunderstanding, that they, too, loved The Dream. They simply had odd and confusing ways of expressing their love.

In the end, The Dream could hear none of it. Too many angry words had slashed its heart and soul. EMTs were incredulous that with so many deep wounds it had survived as long as it had.

We mourners are in shock. Grief overwhelms us. With The Dream's passing, we are no longer the "shining city on a hill," a mecca of opportunity for all who seek it. We are no longer inspired to reach beyond our grasp for the best we can imagine. Bobby Kennedy's immortal words seem like quaint and jarring anachronisms. "Some men see things the way they are and ask why? I dream of things that never were and ask why not?'"

Our Dream had become a shrunken, atrophied, faint shadow of its former lofty grandeur. Our great social compact had fallen casualty to narrow self-centered pursuits. We no longer accepted our obligation to care for "the least of these."

Has a cannibalizing madness now overtaken and infected our body politic? Are we witnessing a viral type of class genocide? Perhaps it is fundamentally suicidal. Maybe the best that tomorrow's obituary can say about our family's dead Dream is that at the ripe old age of 235 years, The Dream had a pretty good run and was finally exhausted.

There is a little known and poorly understood back story to The Dream's demise. Prior to its admission to ICU, it had

AMERICAN POLITICS | *A Death in the Family*

been the victim of a shocking, violent street crime. A mob of callous and calculating estranged family members, having lain in wait and pretending to be its protectors, battered and crippled The Dream. The attackers contended that they were really just trying to protect it. In their defense, they argued that the aging Dream's caregiver (derisively nicknamed "Big Government") had poorly managed The Dream's finances. For The Dream's own protection and survival, they insisted that they had simply intended to force it to live within its means. However, learning of its oft-stated intention to "starve the beast," the people refused to accept the mob's defense. A protective order was issued, forbidding future mob contact with The Dream. The damage, however, had been done. The battered Dream was beyond recovery and restoration.

As we mourn the loss of our precious Dream, the specter of descent into darkness becomes all the more real, for we are nothing without our dreams. An adaptation of Pastor Martin Niemöller's famous Nazi-era cautionary words again comes to mind.

> *They came first for the union workers,*
> *and I didn't speak up because I wasn't a union worker.*
> *Then they came for the teachers,*
> *and I didn't speak up because I wasn't a teacher.*
> *Then they came for the firefighters,*
> *and I didn't speak up because I wasn't a firefighter.*
> *Then they came for me,*
> *and by that time no one was left to speak up.*

Our young leader spoke of resurrecting our revered American dream. Will we mourners follow his lead and bring The Dream back to life?

Send in the Clowns

I was astonished. I used to think that Democrats attract-
ed all the artistic/creative types in politics. But Republicans
showed amazing creativity and artistry in the production of a
Broadway-bound, full-length musical-comedy version of the
2012 contest for president.

They produced an inspired adaptation of the much-
loved Stephen Sondheim song, "Send in the Clowns." In a
flash of artistic genius, Republicans demonstrated their ability as entertainers par excellence, adapting Sondheim's song to
hilarious political parody. Indeed, they transformed the 2012
presidential nominating contest into live comedy, bringing
Republican politicians to the national stage, flawlessly por-
trayed as clowns. Bravo!

Though they were still working out the kinks, this
amazing Republican musical unfolded in close parallel with
Sondheim's song. Follow along with me.

Don't you love farce?

The Republican "loyal opposition" cast had this part
nailed. Could their script be thought of as anything but farce?
Didn't they show remarkable natural talent for ultimate boffo
slapstick?

An earlier version of this essay appeared in the Op-Ed pages of *The Taos News* on
August 4, 2011.

My fault I fear.

The show interpreted national political struggles with exquisite theatrical sensitivity. Supplanting earlier classic theater roles of the warring Jets and Sharks tribes of *West Side Story* fame, here we had decency-deficient, compassion-challenged Republican "Reactionary Regals" (the R's) versus hapless, courage-compromised Democrat "Defeatist Dupes" (the D's).

I thought that you'd want what I want.

In the midst of sidesplitting comedy, talented Republican writers and actors introduced a major theme of tragic horror. Unanticipated, the national ensemble appearance of Republican cast members in social safety net–shredding, public education–starving, union-busting, middle class–destroying roles alarmed early audiences in Middle America. Republican playwrights presumed that American audiences would resonate with the cast portrayal of the solution to the burgeoning national debt on the backs of the halt, the lame, and the infirm. The script appears to be undergoing a major rewrite.

Sorry, my dear.

Well, never mind. In response to a flurry of negative early reviews, writers and producers reprised Gilda Radner's old "Saturday Night Live" character, Emily Litella, as played by Michelle Bachmann ("Miss Mindless"). Bachmann had an uncanny Litella-like ability to be totally divorced from reality. Associated insightful stage direction had the rest of the Republican cast stealthily backing away from Dickensian lines originally delivered by Darth Vader mimic Paul Ryan ("The Predator").

But where are the clowns?

The casting of Republicans who jockeyed to oppose President Obama in 2012 as clowns was impeccable. The production did not have far to look for natural talent for the ensemble clown scenes. It was knee deep in clownish talent. Players Palin, Perry, Bachmann, Trump, Romney, Santorum, and Gingrich were widely acclaimed for their extraordinary gifts as pretenders, court jesters, entertainers, and fools.

Quick, send in the clowns.

In breathtaking breach of plot-line believability, the cast chorus ("Fox News") recited actual Republican presidential candidate names absent uncontrolled hysterics and with dead-pan theatric discipline.

Don't bother, they're here.

As the curtain came down, Mitt Romney delivered the show's powerful final "straight" lines. In the lead role as "Plastic Man," he declared, "There shall be no bread for the poor. Let there be circus instead."

Even now, a dramatic Republican Kafkaesque sequel is in the works. It's based on the words of Texas football legend Darrell Royal, who famously compared a rival team to a bunch of cockroaches: "It's not what they eat and tote off, it's what they fall into and mess up that hurts."

Meanwhile, inspired by the combination of Kafka and Royal, we saw the clownish cast of buggy, tea-partying Republicans pursuing their highest talent and noble purpose: comic entertainment for the masses. What a gift!

The "2012 Republican Follies" opened in New Hampshire and Iowa replete with remarkable clown talent. Watching a televised preview, I laughed so hard I thought I would cry. Republican musical comedy keeps reverberating in my consciousness, bringing a smile to my face, a song to my lips, and doubled-over laughter to my belly.

"Break a leg," Republicans. Thanks for the memories.

Food Fight!

I thought I had already witnessed the height of Republican talent and creativity. Their reprise of the Broadway musical "Send in the Clowns," otherwise known as the GOP presidential nominating contest, left national audiences rolling in the aisles. Nevertheless, it is clear that this cast of talented Republican comics is destined for much bigger things. A hit movie is surely in their future.

The Republicans' endless 2012 nominating road show amply demonstrated their unusual capacity for a remake of the uproarious 1978 comedy *National Lampoon's Animal House.* These Republican characters could easily do *Animal House* in their sleep. Indeed, they were already doing it.

First, we had Newt Gingrich, perfectly cast in the late John Belushi's *Animal House* role. Gingrich's John "Bluto" Blutarsky was awesome, nothing short of superb. Could anyone have rivaled him in this part?

Republican loyalist-cum-drama-critic Peggy Noonan reviewed Gingrich's spectacular natural talent and perfect fit for the role in these words: "He is a human hand grenade who walks around with his hand on the pin, saying, 'Watch this!'"

An earlier version of this essay appeared in the Op-Ed pages of *The Taos News* on February 16, 2012.

Watch this, indeed! We could not take our eyes off his career-capping performance. It was as if Gingrich was channeling Belushi. He has an obviously bright future on the silver screen. He might amass even more money making Hollywood films than doing Washington, D.C., non-lobbying lobbying.

And Gingrich was not alone in demonstrating comedic talent. Other prominent Republican candidates also played major comedic parts.

Could anyone other than Wilbur "Mitt" Romney have been more perfectly cast in the *Animal House* role of Douglas C. Neidermeyer, ROTC cadet officer and military family scion? Neidermeyer was roundly despised, even by his own fraternity brothers. In the film's epilogue, we were told that he was eventually "fragged" (killed by his own troops) in Vietnam. Wasn't this what the Tea Party fraternity had been trying to do to Romney all season? It may be typecasting, but it was brilliantly performed and totally on point. Romney flawlessly played the fraternity brother most Republicans love to hate.

Often identified by male pundits as among the sexiest of Republican women political figures, Michelle Bachmann was superb in a combination of female roles of her wistful admirers' fondest dreams. Repressed Republican men made no secret of their lusty feelings toward this lone Republican woman presidential candidate. (Sorry, guys, Sister Sarah was still playing hard to get.)

In this modern movie remake, Bachmann was a container for projected Republican male fantasies. Here, finally, was a plausible explanation for her continued presence on the national Republican stage. The winsome Bachmann evoked fantasies of a seething inner vamp. Playing against conservative type, she was transformed into the hottie for which her Republican male admirers ambivalently yearn.

Brilliant makeup and costuming allowed Bachmann to take on multiple movie roles, playing directly to these repressed desires. Deft, conservative business attire had her flying under the radar of ever-vigilant Republican wives.

In successive projected fantasies, Bachmann was able to play the dean's lecherous alcoholic wife, Marion. Then she could take on the role of the precocious 13-year-old Clorette. Finally she could become Barbara Sue ("Babs") Jansen, a Southern belle who is indecently exposed in public by the male fraternity brothers. Hadn't Bachmann already been brilliant in the debate scenes containing indecent intellectual exposure? This was a trifecta tour de force of steamy roles, resonating with Bachmann's male admirers' deepest desires.

As with the original production, the Republican remake built to an early boffo high point in its classic food-fight scenes. In an astute nod to current affairs, the updated production moved the setting from campus cafeteria to a series of pretend presidential-candidate debates. Once the mock debates began, all conservative decorum ceased, and it was the side-splitting *Animal House* food fight all over again. Here, bizarre, comic, pelting verbal attacks substituted for the arguably more primitive food hurling of yore. Gingrich's Bluto called out Romney's Neidermeyer, while Bachmann's Marion/Clorette/Babs plaintively interjected zany, mindless, steamy subtext, effectively stealing the show.

Our hats are off to these creative Republicans. Yet again, they offered unmatched circus for the masses.

Little Boy Lost

Once upon a time not so very long ago, there was a sad and lonely little boy. People surrounded him, yet he could never really make and keep good friends. Although people acted as if they were his friends, he had to be constantly entertaining for them to stick around.

Friendship with girls was especially difficult for him. He often said things that hurt their feelings and made them mad. He had seen other boys tease girls and playfully call them names. Some of those boys told him that girls liked it when boys poked fun at them. Whenever he tried it, girls just got angry and didn't want to be his friends anymore. This made him especially sad.

The boy was from a wealthy family that gave him a very big allowance. He sometimes gave part of his allowance to girls who were good at make-believe. He did this in order to get them to pretend to like him and to be his friends. Once he stopped giving them money, they quit being his friends. That hurt his feelings and made him want to get back at them.

The boy's family owned many radio stations. That's how they got to be so rich. In order to take his mind off of

---

An earlier version of this essay, inspired by a national radio host's attack on a young female Georgetown law student, appeared in the Op-Ed pages of *The Taos News* on March 22, 2012.

not having any really good friends, they often let him come down to the radio station and play with the microphones. He liked to talk and entertain people. They thought that this would keep him busy and out of trouble. Although he was a big boy and people expected him to act grown up, he was quite insecure and wanted people to pay a lot of attention to him. He would often say things into the microphones that made people very angry.

Some tried to tell the boy why they were angry about the things he said. He just couldn't understand. It was his family's radio station, and he thought he could say whatever he pleased. If people didn't like it, too bad. When they got angry with him, he often said things that made them even angrier.

The boy's family didn't know what to do with him. They had given him everything he wanted to prove they loved him. When he misbehaved, which was often, they always made excuses for him. He got the wrong idea from this. He got to thinking that it was OK for him to do anything he pleased. He knew he could count on his family to defend him and to explain why whatever he did was just fine.

One day the boy noticed a much younger and smaller girl on TV. She was getting a lot of attention. People said how smart the girl was and what a good job she did talking to these important adults. The boy thought it would be loads of fun to call her really bad names into his family radio station's microphone. He had done this sort of thing before and some people laughed their heads off. He rushed to the microphone and said some of the worst words a boy could say about a girl.

This time hardly anybody laughed. Instead, they said that he was a bully and a coward for picking on a much smaller and younger girl. They said they never again wanted to be his friend. Many boys who earlier thought it fun to tease girls stuck up for the little girl. Although girls are often especially kind, they told him that if he were the only boy on Earth, they would never again be his friends.

The outcome of the story is uncertain. Some say that although the boy was a talented talker, he could not voice the simple words, "I'm sorry." Others say that people who had always listened to his words now wanted simply to hear the two words he was unable to speak. Rumor had it that even the girls with whom he had shared his big allowance would no longer pretend to be his friends.

Anguished and confused, the boy became more and more sad, lonely and lost. Fewer and fewer people now listen to his words. The boy remained a bully, but with an ever-shrinking pulpit.

Of Makers, Takers, and Unawakers

Once upon a time, there was a vast, magnificent, abundant land inhabited by people of three indigenous tribes. The tribes were known as Makers, Takers, and Unawakers (Un-uh-wake-urs).

Makers were principally known for their belief in enormous, individual, unassisted accomplishment. They took extreme umbrage at the mere suggestion that they had not in fact built things totally on their own. Makers bestowed the name "Takers" upon their historic rivals, declaring that these adversaries selfishly sought to benefit from the achievements of others.

Unawakers were defined by their remarkable ability to remain asleep for four-year periods of time. During these long slumbers they were stunningly unaware of the conflicts between the other tribes. Nevertheless, Unawakers, it was widely understood, held the balance of power in the land.

Revered ancestors had long ago decreed that every four years there would be a great contest for the honor of leading the people of the blessed land. Makers had become increas-

An earlier version of this essay appeared in the Op-Ed pages of *The Taos News* on December 6, 2012.

ingly frightened and suspicious. They declared that continued leadership of the handsome, young, eloquent, charismatic Taker Chief would result in ruin.

Aided by a stunningly wealthy roving band of brothers, Makers prophesied that the people would regret their decision to follow the charming Taker Chief. Makers had received this wisdom both from their revered Oracle of Ayn and her acolyte soothsayers, as well as from dire forewarnings from the Faux Fulminating Fox.

Terrified Maker elders loudly proclaimed a plan that they contended would save the long-suffering people. The scheme had come to them in a gilded vision from another age, an era of great misery for ordinary people and astonishing comfort for Makers. Their plan was based on the belief that great sacrifice on the part of ordinary people, combined with extraordinary offerings to the Maker elite, would assure everlasting good fortune for all. The people, however, had vast experience with public sanitation, and called the Maker plan the "Tainted Things Trickle and Flow Downhill" strategy.

No matter how hard Maker leaders tried to convince people of the soundness of their vision, Unawakers viewed the Maker plan with suspicion. As children, Unawakers had learned basic arithmetic in their public schools. They kept telling the Maker tribe's ruling council that the plan's numbers just didn't add up.

In time, Unawakers turned away from the Maker prophesies. They told Maker scouts that they preferred the hopeful, compassionate, inclusive vision of the much maligned leader of the ruling Taker tribe.

Makers had great difficulty hearing the voice of the people above the taxing din and siren song of their prophets. Whenever messengers came to Maker war councils to tell of Unawakers' fondness for the dream of the Taker Chief, the messengers were declared heretics and blasphemers and were immediately banished from the tribe. Despite the devastating storm plainly gathering just over the horizon, the Maker war council continued to insist that Makers would emerge victorious in the end.

And so it came to pass that on the day decreed by the Ancients for great battles between rival tribes of would-be rulers, the Takers achieved a resounding victory. Unawakers followed them and embraced the Taker Chief's vision as their own. The Taker victory was cheered and celebrated far and wide, but not in the councils of Maker elders.

Makers were stunned and shocked beyond belief at the outcome of the great battle. They had been blind to the likely result, though it had been clearly predicted for all who were willing to see and hear. But Makers had refused to see or hear. Some say they just closed their eyes; put their fingers in their ears, and threatened to hold their breath until they turned blue and saw red. Preferring feelings to facts, they swaddled themselves in the illusory comfort of dogma and factually unmoored belief.

For guidance, Maker wise men labored for long hours to decipher a message contained in recently discovered primeval tablets. The words engraved upon the ancient tablets seemed to read, "There are none so blind as those who will not see." It remained unclear as to whether sight would ever be restored to the blind eyes or hearing restored to the deaf ears of Maker chiefs. Only time would tell.

As for the Takers, they ultimately embraced the name that had been disparagingly bestowed upon them. They were indeed "takers," as they did take to heart, take on as their own, and take responsibility for bringing the people's highest hopes and dreams to fruition.

Meanwhile, Unawakers were observed quietly preparing for their impending four-year sleep.

A Lone Profile in Courage

On rare occasions, something admirable and celebratory emerges from our chaotic American political process. Such a "blue moon" phenomenon occurred astronomically and legislatively in the last days of 2009. It may have been easy to miss.

The nation looked on in frustration and disgust as the Republican Party of "NO" and the Democratic Party of "NO COURAGE" struggled through month after month of political stalemate and self-serving posturing over access to necessary health care. This legislative theater of the absurd consistently played to the worst fearful and withholding instincts of the American people, while our citizens continued to suffer and die for want of adequate medical care.

Then something surprising and courageous emerged through the fog. No, it wasn't the actual legislation that eventually received the required number of affirmative Senate votes. There isn't enough to fully celebrate in this lobbyist-directed, -controlled, and -purchased result. The final outcome was politically possible, but not nearly as sweeping as had been hoped.

The unexpected emerged in the form of a lone, brave, quiet voice, whispering above the din of a Congressional

An earlier version of this essay appeared in the Op-Ed pages of *The Taos News* on January 14, 2010.

wasteland of political opportunism and transparent self-interest. Though sometimes derided as a weak leader, Harry Reid came before media microphones day after day, monotonic demeanor and all, an unlikely candidate for this prime time–TV role, softly insisting that some form of health-care legislation *would* pass out of the U.S. Senate. And he kept his promise to the American people. The Senate did pass a version of "reform" legislation, however flawed and disappointing it may be.

Commentators have both lauded and denigrated Senator Reid's achievement in shepherding this health-care measure through the minefield of the U.S. Senate. It was, in fact, accomplished in the face of total Republican opposition.

I must acknowledge my own tepid reaction to the bill's content and my deep disappointment in Congress's failure to enact anything approaching universal care, free of insurance-industry extortion. How can our nation assure access to lawyers for those accused of criminal offenses (as well it should) yet not ensure access to doctors for those in ill health?

Nevertheless, tactical acumen isn't the part of the story worth noting or celebrating. No, the truly admirable was Reid's ability to act nobly and courageously against his own self-interest and in the best interests of his country.

Despite current criticism of him, I stand in awe of Reid's heroism. Once in a long while, someone comes along who takes you totally by surprise. Who knew that this Mister Rogers–like character would turn out to be a hero? He neither looks nor speaks like a credible candidate for the role. There's no way to tell from his TV demeanor that in his youth he was a prizefighter. He seems more like a Sunday-school teacher or modern-day American Gothic artist's model. Yet, he may well be the rare current example of a courageous U.S. senator. Here is a man who voluntarily took a political bullet for his president, for his party, and for the American People.

For this, Senator Reid's reelection prospects seemed dim. He was, after all, on the wrong side of Nevada public opinion. Surprisingly, in perhaps another blue-moon event, he was returned to office. Perhaps some good deeds actually do go unpunished.

A Bay of Pigs Awakening

Once upon a time in America, not so very long ago, a young, handsome, eloquent, intelligent, charismatic U.S. senator was elected president. Surrounded by the best and the brightest of counselors, he was advised that military action to free an oppressed people would result in near certain success. The advisors, as it turned out, were catastrophically wrong, and the military adventure was an unmitigated failure.

That president was, of course, John F. Kennedy, and the military action that he ordered, based on this tragically flawed advice, was the Cuban Bay of Pigs disaster. From this early failure, Kennedy was said to have developed a healthy skepticism for the received wisdom of his "brilliant" advisors. Many believe that, had he lived, he would have questioned their subsequent confident judgments and would have avoided the calamity that lay ahead in Vietnam.

In Barack Obama, we have yet another young, handsome, eloquent, intelligent, charismatic American president. His first-term diffident leadership may also have been shaped by the respected wise men around him. They too may have pressed flawed advice upon their patron.

An earlier version of this essay appeared in the Op-Ed pages of *The Taos News* on February 11, 2010.

President Obama's callow leadership left some of his most ardent supporters deeply disaffected. I voted for President Obama, campaigned for President Obama, and contributed money to President Obama's cause. I have been among the disappointed.

Let us hope that in his futile attempts to find common ground with his opponents, the president has experienced his own "Bay of Pigs" awakening. In any event, we simply cannot allow the president's ongoing political education to be the death of vital social-safety-net programs. Lives depend upon it.

I have certainly not given up on President Obama. Yet I am apprehensive about his initial natural aversion to aggressive leadership in tackling the moral and policy imperatives of our time. Even in actively supporting his run for the presidency, I harbored reservations about his coolness, the absence of any apparent fire in his belly, his true capacity to fight for our shared principles. Despite his early second-term assertiveness, I wonder about this still.

In another time, oppressed minorities demonstrated in the streets and town squares of our country, protesting their deprivation for the entire nation and the whole world to see. The more fortunate among us must now be voices of protest on their behalf, bearing unrelenting public witness to their dire plight. Our fidelity to our nation's highest ideals depends on it. Indeed, the decency and basic humanity of our society will doubtless ultimately be measured by the depth of our concern for the weak and the suffering among us.

President Obama's instinct for collaboration and conciliation is generally laudable. However, in directly calling out obstructionist Republican congressional critics on their distorting, disingenuous, and dissembling political tactics, he may at last demonstrate that he understands the adage that "You don't come to a knife fight unarmed." Perhaps he has the capacity for necessary combat after all.

Hopefully, the obstruction of many of his first-term initiatives has registered with our president as his Bay of Pigs wake-up call. He now speaks of fighting for our most sacred national dreams. Let's hope so.

Budget-Busting "Obamacare"

As President Obama struggled to enact health insurance reform, my conservative friends persistently voiced alarm over the prospect of such legislation. They derided the initiative as "Obamacare" and expressed dire concern over its potential high cost. Their greatest distress seemed the financial burden they fear their grandchildren will inherit.

My friends' concerns for future generations are understandable. They love their grandchildren and want to leave a generous legacy for them. Having listened to their apprehensions, I have a few questions for my tormented friends.

Would you, the budget-troubled insured, personally forego your own costly health care in the interest of increased national fiscal solvency? If not, how do you justify requiring this sacrifice of others?

As beneficiaries of government-run Medicare and Veterans Administration health-care programs, would you really have railed against the catastrophe of a "government takeover" of our national health care? Government-tainted as your own health care is, would you decline it? Wouldn't your grandchildren be confused and troubled by such inconsistency?

An earlier version of this essay appeared in the Op-Ed pages of *The Taos News* on March 25, 2010.

Wouldn't you, in effect, be telling your grandchildren that since you had yours, you were unmoved by the plight of millions of unfortunate uninsured? Does it come down to a matter of "Last one up, pull up the ladder"?

Are you willing to tell your grandchildren that the certain suffering and deaths of additional tens of thousands of uninsured Americans was preferable to their own possibly increased future tax burdens? Would you have told your grandchildren that, in opposing the necessary financing for the uninsured, you valued their financial comfort above the lives of the uninsured parents of some of their friends and acquaintances?

Isn't the allocation of money ultimately a powerful symbolic statement of our country's values? Don't we somehow manage to find the money to do the things in which our nation is invested, such as invade a country that has not attacked us, give disproportionate tax cuts to the wealthiest among us, rescue banks we deem too big to fail?

Given your respect for moral principle, I assume that you will impart to your grandchildren the wisdom and the moral guidance of our civilization's most universally venerated prophets, those whose teachings you hold dear. Wouldn't these very moral pillars have stood in solidarity with the afflicted and against narrow financial self-interest?

As patriotic people, how would you have explained to your grandchildren that our nation's founding fathers pledged their lives, their fortunes, and their sacred honors in the cause of our collective right to "life, liberty, and the pursuit of happiness," but that we, current-day beneficiaries of their vast courageous sacrifices, weren't really committed to the "life" part of their legacy for all Americans?

It remains uncertain if Obamacare will be fully and faithfully implemented. Nevertheless, I wonder still what your responses would be. I am mystified. I don't understand. I know you to be personally kind, caring, and generous people. What am I missing?

Perhaps in the end it's all about money after all. Though we usually try to put a logical face on it, money rarely turns out to be a simple question of logic. It's inevitably an emotionally charged, complex issue that takes on an alternative reality of its own.

It may be that my worried friends are so shaken by the perils of these unsteady economic times that the abstract principle of a national commitment to a universal-health-care dream is unimaginable, no matter what the supporting logic or morality. Maybe the notion of a principled stand on behalf of the uninsured is just too much of a stretch for them, given their own abiding anxieties regarding their current financial well-being.

Fear complicates and compromises the best instincts of good and generous people. We all know fear. It inevitably trumps facts. But we must find the means to overcome this particular fear, for the sake of our suffering fellow Americans, for our nation's most lofty dreams, and for our country's heart and soul. We must do this not just for them but also for ourselves.

Raise My Taxes... Please!

As bizarre as this may seem, I'm not opposed to having my taxes raised. The current zeitgeist, however, clearly reflects the opposite sentiment. There is a clamoring for lower taxes in some circles, especially among the greatest beneficiaries of our nation's largess. Nevertheless, I wish that the government would actually raise my income taxes. Ironically, multibillionaire Warren Buffet and I seem to agree on this.

Yes, raise my taxes, but do not squander, waste, or misappropriate my money. I feel blessed to have an income that obliges me to pay taxes. All I ask is that my income taxes be used wisely and well, in the service of our genuine national interests.

It may be a quaint belief that paying taxes is a sacred responsibility of citizenship in our magnificent nation. Along with many millions of others, an accident of birth bestowed upon me the supreme good fortune of U. S. citizenship. Consequently, I have received many gifts that accrue to those of us who are thus blessed. I am everlastingly grateful for these gifts. I know I'll never adequately repay my country for the bounty that U.S. citizenship has granted me.

An earlier version of this essay appeared in the Op-Ed pages of *The Taos News* on August 26, 2010.

My sentiments stem from a history shared by untold numbers of Americans. Three of my grandparents were early-twentieth-century immigrants to this country. My father was a lifelong factory worker. I grew up in The Bronx. The gifts associated with U.S. citizenship have taken me far from my origins. Indeed, I have lived the proverbial "American dream." I owe this country a great deal, and I am morally bound to repay her investment in me.

I imagine my conservative friends' response: "Nobody did it for you." This is only partially true. I did take advantage of opportunities that came my way. But it is also true that at critical points, both my country and benevolent individuals extended helping hands. I am honor-bound to offer no less to my fellow citizens. My taxes appear the most obvious means to accomplish this.

My conservative friends contend that they are essentially self-made people. This collective mythology asserts that through sheer force of will, personal discipline, and wise decisions, they created their own good fortune. They may actually believe this. I doubt that it is so.

An old friend shared a bit of apropos folk wisdom with me: "When you find a turtle on a fence post, it didn't get there on its own." So it is with us human "turtles." None of us climbed to the top of our fence posts on our own.

My career in psychology has afforded me close contact with the most intimate aspects of the lives of a large and varied group of people, many of them highly successful. This rare, up-close opportunity to know the inner lives of others persuades me that no one is self-made. All of us have been helped along the way. No one, as the poet said, is an "island."

Perhaps this begs the question, where should we turn for help — to government or to private charities? I benefited greatly from government programs of the time that were the fabric of our American social compact. They provided free college tuition and graduate school fellowships and loans. Without them, my career progress would have been much less certain. My assumed obligation was to repay my country's investment in me. Even if charity were personally acceptable and available, charitable resources are nowhere near sufficient to serve our vast national need.

As for tax revenues, money is seldom a matter of logic. Witness greed and fear that overwhelmingly propel our stock markets. Ultimately, money is always a complicated and convoluted psychological symbol, infused with very different meanings for different people.

My conservative friends maintain that the current level of our national debt presages the impending demise of our nation. If they are correct, immediate, dramatic, concerted action is imperative.

The bill has now come due. We who have benefited from the generosity of our great nation must belly up to the bar and put aside our ineffectual hand-wringing. Should we fail to shoulder our responsibilities, who will?

So, raise my taxes — please! Do it now.

Be Very Afraid!

Tea Party founding fathers have succeeded in emptying a terrifying Pandora's Box of inchoate rage into our national politics. This will not end well. Reckless demagogues have released an evil genie that may not be put back in its bottle anytime soon. They are playing a dangerous game, with predictably destructive consequences.

What worries me so about the Tea Party is not just that their candidates may reach elective office, though that's an unfortunate potential outcome. Elections, imperfect as they may be, are our American way. Rather, I'm concerned that unstable or misguided individuals will be unable to distinguish between merely outrageous Tea Party talk and a call to lethal action.

Having practiced psychology for more than 40 years, I have dealt with some very disturbed and imprudent people. Contrary to popular mythology, people suffering serious mental disorders generally have more to fear from us than we have to fear from them. They are typically deeply tortured souls, more vulnerable than menacing. The rare combination of insanity and violent proclivity is, however, capable of monumental lethality.

An earlier version of this essay appeared in the Op-Ed pages of *The Santa Fe New Mexican*, November 7, 2010.

While there may be some truth to the claim that the Tea Party is too diverse to categorize, available data suggest that its adherents largely constitute an extreme element of the Republican Party. I can only hope that my Republican friends will feel seriously moved to put national interest above fleeting political advantage and will rein in this potentially dangerous sub-group.

It is approximately 15 years since misguided "super patriots" blew up the Federal Building in Oklahoma City. In the aftermath of that mass homicide, I treated one of its emotional casualties, a federal agent whose protracted assignment was to identify the body parts of his murdered friends and colleagues. Although he was one of the survivors, he may never be truly whole. What I saw through his eyes will haunt me forever. Let us not repeat such history.

Decent, honorable, patriotic Republicans must "call out" the dangerously misguided in their midst before it's too late. I know they wouldn't want the blood of fellow Americans on their hands.

This is no easy thing. It requires great courage to speak out against the actions of one's own "tribe." In doing so, you risk potential ostracism. Colluding with a wrongheaded course of action is often a more natural path to take. Nevertheless we must all speak up in the name of political sanity, comity, and peace.

Can Words Kill?

"We didn't do anything." "They started it." "They did it more." "They did worse." The words sound eerily like the grade-school protests of our childhoods.

Our teachers would reprimand us for some transgression, and familiar absolution-seeking words would reflexively pour forth. But our childhood denials inevitably fell upon deaf ears. No matter the history or the provocation, and regardless of who did what to whom, we were all responsible.

In the wake of the January 2011, Tucson shooting of U.S. Representative Gabrielle Giffords and 18 others, politicians and pundits were quick to point fingers and deny culpability. It is both ironic and alarming to hear supposed grownups parroting our childhood rationalizations. "The Tea Party did it." "Talk radio did it." "Cable news did it." "The liberals did it." In the end, perhaps we all did it.

What are we to make of the Tucson tragedy? The most comforting conclusion is that this was the act of a lone, deranged gunman. He, and he alone, is responsible for this mass murder and attempted political assassination. The rest of us are blameless. In a purely legal sense, this is undoubtedly true.

An earlier version of this essay appeared in the Op-Ed pages of *The Taos News* on March 3, 2011.

It may be reassuring to think that this was an isolated insane act perpetrated by an individual who bears no resemblance to us, an abominably "bad apple." We've dodged the bullet of culpability.

This seductive conclusion is complicated, however, by an annoying fact: Tucson was not unique. It was just one in a series of horrifying acts of ideologically driven violence afflicting our body politic. A few earlier instances come readily to mind.

- *July 27, 2008:* An armed intruder killed two parishioners and wounded seven in Knoxville's Tennessee Valley Unitarian Universalist Church. The alleged shooter's writings proclaimed his hatred of "the liberal movement." In his home, police found the writings of vociferous right-wing critics Michael Savage, Sean Hannity, and Bill O'Reilly.
- *May 31, 2009:* George Tiller, M.D., Wichita, Kansas OB-GYN, regularly vilified by Bill O'Reilly as "Tiller the killer," was shot to death by an anti-abortion ideologue.
- *June 10, 2009:* A white supremacist, expressing hatred of "liberals in general," opened fire at the U.S. Holocaust Memorial Museum in Washington, D.C. A wounded guard later died of his gunshot injuries.

As a citizen and a psychologist, I had voiced my concern about the potentially lethal combination of mental illness and violent political rhetoric just months before the Tucson massacre in an Op-Ed piece in *The Santa Fe New Mexican* (November 7, 2010). We may never know with certainty what role our overheated political rhetoric may have played in stimulating an individual to mass murder. What we do know is that our political language has reached a fevered and corrosive level. Our words distance us from one another and damage the fiber of our shared humanity. Without question, the constant background drumbeat of vitriol serves no noble purpose. It ultimately weakens our societal bonds, disconnects and separates us from one another, and endangers us all. We must somehow "hush the hate" before it threatens more harm.

In light of the Tucson horror, a psychological defense like projection is especially seductive. It temporarily enables us to deny our personal culpability and to attribute to others our more repulsive human impulses. We can then comfort ourselves in the belief that we don't need to worry any further about such troubling personal impulses. This Tucson massacre was the encapsulated act of an inhuman lunatic. Therefore, we are pure. We are blameless. We bear no responsibility.

While blaming others is psychologically appealing and politically *de rigueur*, the healing of our nation's emotional wounds requires that we own what we have projected onto others. While it would be comforting to pretend reckless rage is the sole province of the Tea Party, that greedy indifference exclusively defines Republicans, or that imprudent overindulgence is private Democratic territory, this would be a grave error. It is more likely that diluted versions of these denied sentiments exist in all of us.

Even at our fellow human being's worst, we are "them" and they are "us." Only in acknowledging our nastiest impulses can we control them and realize the best in us.

Tucson was not unique. Words do matter. We are in this vulnerable national lifeboat together.

Oh, Susana!

Though cold, confused, and concerned, I didn't want Susana to cry for me. Watching our governor's Taos press conference during that time of days-long natural-gas curtailment, I thought she sounded like the New Mexico Gas Company's press secretary. She expressed pride in the generosity and self-reliance of New Mexicans in weathering the crisis.

I wish I could feel similar pride in her emergency leadership. Instead, she offered disappointing explanations and excuses for the company's failure to provide essential utility service. Her modified J.F.K.-type declaration suggested, "Ask not what your [government] can do for you, but what you can do for [yourselves]."

Governor, perhaps you finally heard. It was midwinter in our northern New Mexico mountains. Temperatures here consistently fell below zero; the day the gas was turned off, it reached minus 18. You declared a state of emergency. If decisive actions followed, I must have missed them.

Did I miss your demand that the gas company deploy crews round the clock to urgently restore vital services? When you finally called out the National Guard, did I misunderstand

An earlier version of this essay appeared in the Op-Ed pages of *The Taos News* on February 10, 2011.

the size of the emergency force? Was it 2,500 that you mobilized or 25, as I have been told? Did I not appreciate the stroke of genius that allowed the gas company control of service-restoration information, placing your waiting constituents under virtual house arrest?

You previously declared, "New Mexico is open for business." Was this what you had in mind? Our businesses were largely closed!

Oh, Susana, can you say, "Hurricane Katrina"? How about "BP"?

A Missed Media Moment

As one among many thousands who "weathered" four to six frigid February days of natural gas–service curtailment in Taos and northern New Mexico, I was amazed by the content of *The Santa Fe New Mexican* reporter Kate Nash's February 11, 2011, news item, "Elected officials: Martinez passed test of handling natural gas crisis."

It was a shock that the *New Mexican* would run this as a straight news story, rather than as satire, or as the slanted, revisionist opinion piece that it was.

While the remarks of elected officials are often newsworthy, these were newsworthy mostly in light of how strongly they diverged from constituents' judgments and sentiments. For us, our governor's crisis leadership was an utter failure. We suffered through days without heat during some of winter's most frigid weather. For days our governor did precious little to aid us.

There is surely a real story in this piece of political damage control masquerading as straight news. Quoted officials aside, the piece was literally laced with the reporter's slanted, pro-Martinez opinions presented as fact. This would be fine

---

An earlier version of this essay appeared in the Op-Ed pages of *The Santa Fe New Mexican,* April 18, 2011.

as an Op-Ed piece, but as a straight news story? Clearly, a vital news-versus-opinion boundary had been breached.

If the *New Mexican* does not present the facts, and the governor is not held accountable for failure to act quickly and effectively in an emergency, what will happen next time? There *will* be a next time. To my knowledge, nobody died in this gas curtailment. But what will happen when life-threatening wildfires come again to our region? Will it take four or more long days for the governor to take strong action? And will the *New Mexican* again give the governor an undeserved pass for future crisis leadership failures?

Where Have They Gone?

"Has anybody here seen my old friend Abraham? Can you tell me where he's gone?" These soul-searing lyrics of "Abraham, Martin and John," the 1968 lament for the martyred Lincoln, King, and Kennedys, make our hearts ache. Where, indeed, have they gone?

Though they have undoubtedly been idealized and mythologized over time, where, too, are the inspirational Washingtons, Jeffersons, Franklins, and Roosevelts for our age?

While not without noteworthy flaws, American leaders used to be thought of as giants among our planet's people. We yearn for statesmen who put principle above party and national interest above self-interest. Yet truly courageous leaders are in short supply. Are we doomed to witness the legacy of earlier leadership greatness being passed to moral midgets and political parasites? Where, indeed, have they gone?

How did it come to this? Has our nation's pool of extraordinary leadership talent simply evaporated? Was our earlier American experience a unique epoch, an accident in time? Were these remarkable individuals born leaders for whose very existence we were simply the beneficiaries of

---

An earlier version of this essay appeared in the Op-Ed pages of *The Taos News* on August 8, 2012.

genetic accidents? Alternatively, were these leaders formed in response to historic imperatives, creative human reactions to the gripping national crises of their times?

One theory of leadership development holds that leaders are *made*, not *born*, that we create the leaders we need to carry forward our collective hopes, dreams, and fears. Having now erected the best government that money can buy, we have developed leaders who faithfully mirror who we have now become. Current leaders are exquisitely well suited to pursue narrow interests, effectively portraying a rampage of self-absorption by the prominent and the powerful. Greed has become God.

Politician and social activist Tom Hayden wisely observed that politicians do not lead parades; they follow them. If we truly desire a different ethos, it falls to us to organize the national "parade" that a politician may then step to the head of and "lead."

But what might be the content of the collective expression of our yearnings, the thrust of such a people's parade? Its substance may be hiding in plain sight, embedded in the disparate threads of our unarticulated, inchoate hopes and fears, waiting to be uncovered. Recent widespread, nonviolent "Occupy" demonstrations in pursuit of social justice have given voice to the suffering of many. Could the public face of the leadership we lack be found in this charged medium?

Panderers and pretenders, emissaries and enablers of our bankrupt leadership are ubiquitous. Yet and still, the people possess the capacity to produce a leader of their dreams. They are the empowering force in the creation of a person who might emerge in response to their clear, collective call. It is up to us to demand a society of compassion and inclusiveness, one that functions with scrupulous integrity and fidelity to our highest values, one that keeps faith with the earlier giants who pledged their lives, their fortunes, and their sacred honors in our behalf.

Can our voices be clear and unwavering in rejection of cynical, callous, mean-spirited political attacks that shred our sacred social compact, divide us from our fellow Americans, and assault the most vulnerable among us? Will we reject so-called "leadership" that devolves into decency-destroying, democracy-diminishing darkness? Will we do this for our brothers and sisters — before the forces of fear and their divisions of discord come for and overwhelm us all?

Throughout the nation, the occupy movement and its numerous offshoots bore witness to the plutocracy we have become. Will our elected "leaders" come forward and embrace the interests of the 99 percent?

Across the tortured Middle East, in the Arab Spring, courageous citizens stood in mortal peril, asserting their demands for a modicum of democracy. Can we do any less for ourselves?

At long last, is a true and courageous American leader detectable within the current moral morass? Could such a person emerge through the fog? Could that person be Barack Obama? Is there somewhere a Bobby, a Martin, a John, or a "Jane" for our time? Has anybody here seen my old friend Abraham?

In Conclusion

Sacred Hearts, Sacred Minds, Sacred Dreams

How does one describe a place that can neither be seen nor touched, one that is not about bricks and mortar, nor about a noteworthy geologic site, no matter how beloved or spectacular it may be?

Taoseños cherish their sacred places: the Taos Pueblo and its rich, extensive history and culture; the drama and majesty of the Rio Grande Gorge; the time-honored spiritual traditions of the Saint Francis Church, to name a few. Nevertheless, my personal candidates for Taos's most moving sacred places are all around me, hiding in plain sight. I am surrounded by them. They accompany me with every step I take.

With all due respect to Taos's best-known sacred places, my own most sacred places have little to do with concrete, physical structures. For me, the most sacred Taos places are the enduring and inspiring qualities that reside within the hearts and minds of its people: the enormously talented, creative, insightful, and astonishingly generous natures of those who make Taos their home. I am awed, as I repeatedly discover the boundless reservoir of inventive human thought and rich feeling that infuse and inspire life in Taos. These are ubiquitous sacred places.

I encounter the sacred spirit of Taos in the individual who, though born to great privilege and wealth, is ever mindful of the old adage "To whom much has been given, much is expected." I meet the sacred in the businessperson who draws together individuals across varied political persuasions and cultures in efforts to heal the sick and the suffering, taking care of Taos's own. I discover it again in the joining of indigenous Taoseños with recently arrived "émigrés" in a service organization whose mission is to improve and enrich the lives of its neighbors.

I come upon the sacred in the multi-talented, multi-faceted people who routinely turn out to know far more, do far more, and be far more than might be apparent. I find it in the attorney who is an accomplished performing artist, the auto-repair-shop owner who offers wise personal counsel to an elderly customer, and in the artist who volunteers emergency lifesaving wilderness rescue skills.

Taos's most sacred places exist for me not only in the hearts and minds of the people of Taos but also in the rich and optimistic contents of their dreams. They evoke and recall for me Bobby Kennedy's poignant "dream of things that never were" quote, which seems like a quaint anachronism.

Unconstrained by conventional imaginations, and likely to endure for all eternity, Taos's most sacred dreams reflect the challenge, the opportunity, the exuberance, and the promise of "Why not?" Ultimately, this is where I encounter sacred Taos.

To Stand and Deliver

"Breathtaking," "jaw dropping," "stunning," "magnificent" are words that came immediately to mind that night. This was not my first time hearing them. There had been other times and other places. On each previous occasion, I had thought that it just couldn't get any better than this. Yet much to my surprise and delight, each event had somehow managed to surpass the one before.

Whenever I've heard Taos's high-school poets perform their work I've been awed. Though no longer a new thing, it's a sure thing. Each time has moved and inspired me deeply. That's how it was at a recent program dedicated to the work of young Taos writers.

The Harwood Museum's Arthur Bell Auditorium was the program's venue, its stadium-style seating stretching to the room's rafters. The well-attended event drew a predominantly young audience sprinkled here and there with middle-aged and elderly spoken-word fans. The pre-program anticipatory energy of the teenagers was electric. We were in for the emotional ride of our lives.

Following brief introductions, the program began. All eyes on them, the student writers and poets, each in turn,

An earlier version of this essay appeared in the Op-Ed pages of *The Taos News* on March 14, 2013.

confidently and courageously stood at the unadorned blond-wood podium at the center of the auditorium's stage floor. Urged on by their peers, they looked up toward the enthusiastic gathering gazing down on them. Then, one after the other, they delivered.

And what a delivery it was. Spoken words, at times reinforced with flawless *a cappella* song snippets, flowed from their young mouths, minds, hearts, and souls. The language swooped and soared, careened and caromed, dipped and dove, as evocative images carried us on joyous journeys, through depths of despair to pinnacles of passion.

These young poets held us in rapt attention in their search for meaning in their lives, their quest for love connections, their fierce outrage against violence toward women. The thoughts of these teenagers in our midst were emotionally nuanced, stunningly sophisticated, artfully articulate, and resolutely fearless.

Only verbatim recall of their actual words could adequately communicate their enormous talent. Yet, I was so lost in the moment, so totally entranced by the rich and evocative words and the powerfully authentic themes of these young poets, I'm unable to recall even one of them. It's as if they took me to an altered state.

Though they may lack wisdom born of long life experience, these teenagers possessed compensating abilities to see through fresh eyes and to speak in pure tones. Their talent was a clear reminder of the power of art to penetrate hardened defenses, deepen understanding, and evoke change.

With such staunch young keepers of our collective conscience and stewards of our shared soul, how could we not be optimistic about the future? If they are able to summon the resolve to speak authentically, how can the rest of us not convene the courage to speak our own truths to power? This is a sacred obligation that we too incur toward future generations.

The current state of our nation brings to mind the words of British statesman and philosopher Edmund Burke: "The only thing necessary for evil to triumph is for good men [and women] to do nothing." These words are as relevant today as ever. Failure to speak out, bearing unflinching witness to wrong and extolling the exceptional, is tantamount to aiding and abetting injustice.

With these talented young people as inspiration, how could we not also be willing to speak, to sing, to write, to dance, to march, to hope, and to dream? How could we not let our voices be heard? How could we, in concert with these inspiring high-school students, not also stand and deliver?

About the Work

Tributes and Tirades: Taos Life and American Politics is a collection of commentaries and opinions on events in a troubled period in American politics and life in Taos, a storied northern New Mexico town. Some of the essays are revisions of previously published Op-Ed or literary-anthology pieces. Others appear in print for the first time. Author Robert J. Silver, a psychologist by background and training, was captivated by Taos's legendary transformational power. These collected writings are the result of the magic that is Taos.

About the Author

Following graduation from the City College of New York in 1965, Robert J. Silver left the city of his birth for doctoral study at Indiana University-Bloomington. A four-decade career in clinical and forensic psychology followed, including academic appointments at Illinois State University and The University of Texas-Austin, concurrent with an active clinical and forensic psychology practice (www.robertsilverpsychology.com). He and his wife, abstract painter Dianne Frost, became residents of Taos in 1999, permanently relocating there in 2008. He continues to practice forensic psychology while pursuing his love of creative writing.

www.ingramcontent.com/pod-product-compliance
Lightning Source LLC
Chambersburg PA
CBHW072013040426
42447CB00009B/1611

9780615807997